50 ALL NEW creative discussions for
junior high youth groups

David Lynn

 Youth
Specialties

▧ ZondervanPublishingHouse
A Division of HarperCollins*Publishers*

ZONDERVAN/YOUTH SPECIALTIES BOOKS

Professional Resources

Called to Care
Developing Student Leaders
Feeding Your Forgotten Soul
Growing Up in America
High School Ministry
How to Recruit and Train Volunteer Youth Workers
     (Previously released as Unsung Heroes)
Junior High Ministry (Revised Edition)
The Ministry of Nurture
Organizing Your Youth Ministry
Peer Counseling in Youth Groups
The Youth Minister's Survival Guide
Youth Ministry Nuts and Bolts

Discussion Starter Resources

Get 'Em Talking
Hot Talks
More Junior High TalkSheets
Option Plays

Special Needs and Issues

The Complete Student Missions Handbook
Divorce Recovery for Teenagers
Ideas for Social Action
Intensive Care: Helping Teenagers in Crisis
Up Close and Personal: How to Build Community in
     Your Youth Group

Youth Ministry Programming

Adventure Games
Creative Programming Ideas for Junior High Ministry
Creative Socials and Special Events
Good Clean Fun
Good Clean Fun, Volume 2
Great Games for City Kids
Great Ideas for Small Youth Groups
Greatest Skits on Earth
Greatest Skits on Earth, Volume 2
Holiday Ideas for Youth Groups (Revised Edition)
Junior High Game Nights
More Junior High Game Nights
On-Site: 40 On-Location Youth Programs
Play It! Great Games for Groups
Super Sketches for Youth Ministry
Teaching the Bible Creatively
The Youth Specialties Handbook for Great Camps
     and Retreats

4th-6th Grade Ministry

How to Survive Middle School
Incredible Stories

Clip Art

ArtSource™ Volume 1—Fantastic Activities
ArtSource™ Volume 2—Borders, Symbols, Holidays,
     and Attention Getters
ArtSource™ Volume 3—Sports
ArtSource™ Volume 4—Phrases and Verses
ArtSource™ Volume 5—Amazing Oddities and
     Appalling Images
ArtSource™ Volume 6—Spiritual Topics
Youth Specialties Clip Art Book
Youth Specialties Clip Art Book, Volume 2

Video

Next Time I Fall In Love Video Curriculum
Understanding Your Teenager Video Curriculum
Video Spots for Junior High Game Nights

OTHER BOOKS BY DAVID LYNN

Amazing Tension Getters—with Mike Yaconelli
     (Zondervan/Youth Specialties)
Attention Grabbers for 4th-6th Graders (Zondervan/
     Youth Specialties)
Great Games for 4th-6th Graders (Zondervan/Youth
     Specialties)
Grow For It Journal—with Mike Yaconelli (Zondervan/
     Youth Specialties)
High School TalkSheets (Zondervan/Youth Specialties)
Junior High TalkSheets (Zondervan/Youth Specialties)
More Attention Grabbers for 4th-6th Graders
     (Zondervan/Youth Specialties)
More Great Games for 4th-6th Graders (Zondervan/
     Youth Specialties)
More High School TalkSheets (Zondervan/ Youth
     Specialties)
More Quick and Easy Activities for 4th-6th Graders
     (Zondervan/Youth Specialties)
More Zingers: 25 Real-Life Character Builders
     (Zondervan)
Parent Ministry TalkSheets (Zondervan/Youth
     Specialties)
Rock Talk (Zondervan/Youth Specialties)
Teaching the Truth About Sex—with Mike Yaconelli
     (Zondervan/Youth Specialties)
Tension Getters—with Mike Yaconelli (Zondervan/
     Youth Specialties)
Tension Getters Two—with Mike Yaconelli (Zondervan/
     Youth Specialties)
Twisters: Questions You Never Thought to Ask!
     (Zondervan)
Quick and Easy Activities for 4th-6th Graders
     (Zondervan/Youth Specialties)
Zingers: 25 Real-Life Character Builders (Zondervan)

MORE JUNIOR HIGH TalkSheets

Table of Contents

Table of Contents (continued)

HOW TO USE TALKSHEETS

You have in your possession a very valuable book. It contains 50 instant youth group discussions for junior high school students. Inside you will find reproducible "TalkSheets" covering a wide variety of "hot topics," plus simple step-by-step instructions on how to use them. All you need for 50 successful youth meetings is this book and a copy machine.

TalkSheets are easy to use and are very flexible. They can be used in a youth group meeting, a Sunday school class, or in a Bible study group. They are adaptable for either large or small groups. They can be fully covered in 20 minutes or more intensively in two hours. You can build an entire youth group meeting around a single TalkSheet or you can use TalkSheets to supplement other materials and resources you might be using. The choice is yours.

TalkSheets are much more than just another type of curriculum or workbook. They actually get the students involved and excited about discussing important issues and growing in their faith. Talksheets deal with key topics young people want to talk about. With interesting activities, challenging questions, and eye-catching graphics, TalkSheets will capture the attention of your students and help them think and learn. The more often you use TalkSheets, the more your junior high students will look forward to them.

TALKSHEETS ARE DISCUSSION STARTERS

Although TalkSheets can be used as curricula for your youth group, they are primarily designed to be used as discussion starters. Everyone knows the value of a good discussion. In a discussion, young people take part and interact with one another. When they are talking about a specific subject, they are more apt to do some serious thinking about it, to try to understand it better, to formulate and defend their points of view, and to make decisions. Discussion helps truth rise to the surface and helps young people discover it for themselves. There is no better way to promote learning than to encourage good discussion.

A common fear voiced by many junior high youth group leaders is "What will I do if the students in my group just sit there and don't say a word?" This is why many group leaders would rather show a movie or give a lecture.

Usually when students don't have anything to say, it's because they haven't had the time or the opportunity to get their thoughts organized. Most young people haven't yet developed the ability to "think on their feet." They do not know how to present their ideas and opinions spontaneously, with confidence. They are afraid to open their mouths for fear they might sound stupid.

This is why TalkSheets work so well. TalkSheets give young people a chance to interact with the subject matter in an interesting, challenging, and nonthreatening way, *before* the actual discussion begins. This not only gives them time to organize their thoughts and to write them down, but it also reduces any anxiety they might feel about participating. Most students will actually look forward to sharing their answers and finding out how others respond to the same questions. They will be primed and ready for a lively discussion.

A STEP-BY-STEP USER'S GUIDE

TalkSheets are very easy to use, but they do require a minimum of preparation. Follow these simple instructions and you will have a successful TalkSheet discussion.

Choose the right TalkSheet for your group. Each TalkSheet deals with a different topic. The one you choose will depend upon the needs and the maturity level of your group. Don't feel obligated to use the TalkSheets in the order in which they appear in this book. They were not intended to be used that way.

2 **Try it yourself.** Once you have chosen a TalkSheet for your group, answer the questions and do the activities yourself. Imagine your students' reactions to the TalkSheets. This will give you firsthand knowledge of what you will be asking your students to do. As you fill out the TalkSheet, think of other appropriate questions, activities, and Scriptures.

3 **Read the Leader's Instructions on the back of each TalkSheet.** Included are numerous tips and ideas for getting the most out of your discussion. You may wish to add some of your own thoughts or ideas in the margins. Fill in the date and the name of the group at the top of each leader's page.

4 **Remove the TalkSheet from the book.** The pages are perforated along the left margin for easy removal. Carefully tear out the TalkSheet you have chosen, thereby making it easier to copy. Before you run off copies, you might wish to "white out" (with liquid paper) the page number at the bottom of the TalkSheet.

5 **Make a copy for everyone in the group.** Each student will need his or her own copy of the TalkSheet. This book makes the assumption that you have access to a copy machine. Obviously, you will make copies of only the student's side of the TalkSheet. The leader's material on the other side is just for you, the leader.

Keep in mind that you are able to make copies for your group because we have given you permission to do so. (U.S. copyright laws still mandate that you request permission from a publisher before making copies of any other published material. It is against the law not to do so.) Permission is granted, however, for you to make copies of this material for *your own group only*, not for every youth group in your state. Thank you for cooperating.

6 **Introduce the topic.** In most cases, it is important to introduce, or "set up," the topic before you pass out the TalkSheets to your group. Any method will suffice as long as it is relatively short and to the point. Be careful not to "over introduce" the topic. Be careful not to use an introduction that is too "preachy" or that resolves the issue before you even get started. You want to whet the appetites of the young people—to stretch their minds—and leave plenty of room for discussion. The primary purpose of the introduction is to spark interest in the topic.

The simplest way to introduce the topic is to do so verbally. You can tell a story, share an experience, or describe a situation or problem having to do with the topic. You might wish to evoke responses by asking a simple question, such as "What is the first thing you think of when you hear the word _____ (the topic)? After a few answers have been volunteered, you can reply, "It seems we all have different ideas about this subject. Tonight we are going to investigate it a bit further. . . ." Then pass out the TalkSheet, making certain everyone has a pen or pencil, and you are on your way.

The following ways are excellent methods you can use to introduce any topic in this book:

  a. Show a pertinent short film or video.
  b. Read an interesting passage from a book or a magazine article that relates to the subject.
  c. Play a popular song dealing with the topic.
  d. Perform a short skit or dramatic presentation.
  e. Play a simulation game or "role-play," setting up the topic.
  f. Present some current statistics, survey results, or a current newspaper article that provides recent information about the topic.
  g. Use a crowd breaker or game, getting into the topic in a humorous way.
  h. Use posters, slides, or any other audio-visual aids available to help focus attention on the topic.

There are endless possibilities: How you introduce the topic is entirely up to you. You are limited only by your own creativity. Each TalkSheet offers a few suggestions, but you are free to use any method with which you feel comfortable. Keep in mind that the introduction is a very important part of each session. It will help set the tone and will influence the kinds of responses you get from the students. Don't "load" the introduction to the point that the group knows the "answer" or resolution in advance or the students will not feel free to share their opinions openly and honestly.

7 **Give your students enough time to work on their TalkSheets.** Pass out a copy of the TalkSheet to each member of the group after the introduction. Each person should also have a copy of the Bible, as well as a pen or pencil. There are usually five to six activities on each TalkSheet. If your time is limited, or if you are using only a portion of the TalkSheet to supplement your curriculum, instruct the group to complete only the activities you feel appropriate.

Decide ahead of time whether or not you wish the students to work on their TalkSheets individually or in groups.

Encourage them to consider what the Bible has to say as they complete their TalkSheets.

Give a time limit for completing the TalkSheet and then when there is only a minute or two left to go, let them know. If most kids need more time, allow it, if at all convenient. If most of the students have finished before the time is up, call "time" and begin the discussion.

8 **Lead the discussion.** The next step is to discuss the TalkSheet with the group. If you want to use these worksheets successfully, all members of your group should be encouraged to participate. It is important to foster an atmosphere conducive to discussion by communicating to the students the importance of each person's opinion. It is essential they understand their responsibility to contribute to the discussion. In order for these worksheets to have any meaning, there must be a variety of opinions.

If your youth group is very large, you may wish to divide it into smaller groups of six to 12. Each of these smaller groups should have a facilitator to keep the discussion going. The facilitator can be either an adult leader or a student member. Advise the leaders that they should be on equal footing with the other members of the group. They should not try to dominate the others, and if the group looks to the facilitator for the "answer," ask the facilitator to direct the responses back to the group. Once the smaller groups have completed their discussions, combine them into one large group and go through each of the items again, asking the different groups to summarize what they learned from each activity.

It is not necessary to divide into smaller groups every time you use the TalkSheets. Vary the groups—sometimes utilize only large group discussion, other times use small groups. You may wish, with certain subjects, to divide the meeting into groups of the same sex.

The discussion should concentrate on the questions and answers on the TalkSheet. Go through them one at a time, asking the students to share their responses to each item. Have them compare their answers and brainstorm new ones in addition to the ones they have written down. Those who don't feel comfortable revealing their answers should be allowed to pass on any question.

Don't feel pressured to spend time on every single activity. If times does not permit a discussion on every item, skip those that have evoked the least interest. Focus on those that appear to be the most stimulating to the whole group.

Follow your own creative instinct. If you discover a different way to use the activity, do so. Don't feel bound by the leader's instructions on the back of the TalkSheet. Use Scriptures other than those designated. Add any items that you feel are pertinent. TalkSheets were designed to be open-ended in order for you to be able to add your own thoughts and ideas.

If the group begins to digress about an issue that has nothing to do with the main topic, guide it back on track. If, however, there is a high degree of interest in this "side issue," or if discussing it seems to meet a need of the majority, then you may wish to go ahead and see where the discussion leads. The point is to be as creative and flexible as necessary. (More information on leading discussions can be found in the next section.)

9 **Wrap up the discussion.** This is your chance to present a challenge to the group. When considering your closing remarks, ask yourself the following question: "What do I want the students to remember most from this discussion?" If you can answer in two or three sentences, then you have your closing remarks. It is important to bring some sort of conclusion to the session without negating the thoughts and opinions expressed by the students. A good wrap-up should affirm the group and offer a summary that helps tie the discussion together. Your students should be left with the desire to discuss the issue further, to talk about it with a leader. Tell your group members you are available for private discussion after the session. In some cases, a wrap-up may be unnecessary; just leave the issue hanging and discuss it again at some later date. This will permit your students to think about it longer, on their own, and at a later date the loose ends can be tied up.

10 **Follow up with an additional activity.** The leader's instructions on the back of the TalkSheet provide ideas for additional activities. They are optional but highly recommended. The purpose of these activities is to give the group members the opportunity to reflect upon, evaluate, review, and assimilate what they have learned. Most of your TalkSheet discussions will only whet your students' appetites for further discussion on the subject. These additional activities will lead to more discussion and better learning.

Assign the activity and then follow up with a short debriefing discussion at the next group meeting. The following are good questions to ask about the activity:

   a. What happened when you did this activity? Was it helpful or a waste of time?
   b. How did you feel when you were performing this activity?
   c. Did the activity change your mind or affect you in some way?
   d. In one sentence, state what you learned from this activity.

HOW TO LEAD A TALKSHEET DISCUSSION

The young people of today are growing up in a world of moral confusion. The problem facing youth leaders is not so much teaching the church's beliefs and values as much as it is helping young people make the right choices in a world of so many options. Traditionally, the church's response to this problem has been to indoctrinate—to preach and yell its point of view louder than the rest of the world. Such an approach, however, does not work in today's world. Teenagers are hearing a variety of voices and messages, most of which are louder than those they are hearing from the church.

A TalkSheet discussion works for this very reason. While discussing the questions and activities on the TalkSheet, your youths will be encouraged to think carefully about issues, to compare their beliefs and values with others, and to make discerning choices. TalkSheets will challenge your teenagers to evaluate, defend, explain, and rework their ideas in a Christian atmosphere of acceptance, support, and growth.

CHARACTERISTICS OF A TALKSHEET DISCUSSION

Fruitful discussions—those that produce learning and growth—rarely happen by accident. A successful discussion requires careful preparation and a sensitive leader. Don't be concerned if you think you lack experience or don't have the time to spend lengthy hours in preparation. TalkSheets are designed to help even the novice leader conduct a memorable discussion. The more TalkSheet discussions you lead, the easier it will become. The following information should be extremely helpful. The ideas can be easily incorporated into your TalkSheet discussions.

Create a climate of acceptance. Most teenagers are afraid to express their opinions because they fear being ridiculed, being laughed at, and being considered "dumb" by their peers. They need to feel secure before they share their true feelings and beliefs. They also need to know they can share their thoughts and ideas, even if those are unpopular or "wild." If any of your group members are made to suffer put-downs, criticism, derisive laughter, or judgmental comments—even if their statements are opposed to the teachings of the Bible—an effective discussion cannot be accomplished. For this reason, each TalkSheet begins with a question or activity less threatening and more fun than some of those that follow. The first question helps the students become more comfortable with each other and with the prospect of sharing their ideas.

In order to help you transmit the idea of total acceptance, always phrase your questions—even those that are printed on the TalkSheets—in such a way that you are asking for an *opinion*, not an *answer*. For example, instead of saying, "What should Jessica have done in that situation?" change it to "What **do you think** Jessica should have done in that situation?" The simple addition of the three words "do you think" makes the question less threatening and a matter of opinion, rather than a demand for the "right" answer. When young people realize only their opinions are required, they feel more comfortable and confident. In addition, the idea that a leader actually cares about their opinions on a subject boosts their self-images.

Affirm all legitimate expressions of opinion from your group members. Make certain everyone knows her or his comments and contributions are appreciated and important. This is especially true for those who rarely speak up in group activities. When they do, make a point of thanking them for joining in. This will be an incentive for them to participate further.

Remember, affirmation does not always have to mean approval. Affirm even those comments that seem like heresy to you. By doing so, you inform the group that all have the right to express their ideas, no matter how controversial those ideas may be. If someone does express an opinion that you believe is way off base, make a mental note of the comment. Then, in your concluding remarks, refute the incorrect comment or present an alternative point of view, in a positive way. Do not reprimand the student who voiced the comment.

Discourage the students from thinking of you as the "authority" on the subject. It is typical of students to think you have the "right answer" to every question. They will look to you for approval, even when they are answering another group member's question. If you notice the responses focused primarily on you for this reason, redirect them toward the group by making a comment such as, "Talk to the group, not to me" or "Tell everyone, not just me."

Try to keep your purpose as "facilitator" as strong an image as possible. It is essential your students regard you as a member of the group, on an equal footing with them, whose primary aim is to keep the discussion alive and kicking. You are not sitting in judgment of their responses, nor do you have the correct answer for everything.

Remember, the less of an authority figure you appear to be, the more weight your own opinions will have to your impressionable teenagers. If you are regarded as a friend, they will give more credence to your words. You have a tremendous responsibility to be, with sincerity, their trusted friend.

Actively listen to each person. God gave you one mouth and two ears. Good discussion leaders know how to listen. Your job is not to monopolize the discussion or to put in your two cents worth on each issue. Keep your own mouth shut except when it encourages others to talk. Remember, you are a *facilitator.* You can express your opinions during your concluding remarks.

Do not force anyone to talk. Invite them, but do not insist they comment. Each member needs to have the right to "pass."

Do not take sides during the discussion. You will possibly have differing opinions in the group from time to time. This is very stimulating to a discussion, but do not make the mistake of agreeing with one side or the other. Instead, encourage both sides to think though their positions and to defend their points of view. You might ask probing questions to encourage deeper examination of their opinions. If everyone seems to agree on a question, or if they seem reticent about expressing a controversial opinion, it might be wise to take the other side, playing the devil's advocate with tough questions, forcing them to stretch their thinking even more. Do not leave the impression the "other" point of view is necessarily your own. Remain neutral.

Do not allow one person—including yourself—to monopolize the discussion. Almost every group has one person who likes to talk and is perfectly willing to express an opinion on any subject. Try to encourage equal participation from all the students.

Arrange seating to encourage discussion. "Theater style" seating—in rows—is one of the worst ways to set up chairs for a discussion. If you will be using chairs, arrange them in a circular or semi-circular pattern. If the group is very large or if you notice the students are reluctant to participate, break them up into smaller groups of four to six persons. Have them discuss the questions and share their answers in the smaller group. This format is frequently less threatening to teenagers, especially if they represent a variety of maturity levels. If you have both junior high students and senior high students in the same youth meeting, let them divide up accordingly.

Allow for humor when appropriate. Do not take the discussions so seriously that they cannot be fun. Most TalkSheets include questions designed to generate laughter as well as intense, serious thought.

Don't be intimidated by silence. Silence is sometimes frightening to discussion leaders. Some react by trying to fill in the silence with a question or a comment. The following suggestions may help you handle silence more effectively:

a. Learn to feel comfortable with silence. Wait it out for 30 seconds. Give someone a reasonable time to respond. If you feel it is appropriate, designate someone to comment. Sometimes a gentle nudge is all that is needed.

b. Discuss the silence with the group. Ask the students what the silence really means. Perhaps they are confused or embarrassed and don't feel free to share.

c. Answer the silence with questions or comments about it, such as "I know this is a difficult issue to consider . . ." or "It's scary to be the first to talk." Acknowledging the silence in this manner may break the ice.

d. Ask a different question that might be easier to handle or that might clarify the one already posed. But do not do this too quickly. Wait first.

Try to keep the discussion under control. It is common for a discussion to become sidetracked. You may not want the digression to continue.

If one of the group members brings up a side issue that seems to generate a lot of interest and discussion, you will need to decide whether or not to pursue it or whether to redirect the discussion back to the original topic. If the interest is strong and the issue is worth discussion, sometimes the digression can be valuable. In most cases, however, it is advisable to say something like "Let's come back to that subject a little later if we have the time. Right now, let's finish our discussion on. . . ."

Be creative and flexible. Do not feel pressured to follow the order of the questions on the TalkSheet. If you wish, use only a couple of them or add a few of your own. The leader's guide on the back of the TalkSheet may give you some ideas, but think of your own as well. Each question or activity may lead to others along the same lines that you can bring up during the discussion.

Be an "askable" discussion leader. Try to communicate to the students they can feel free to talk with you about anything, with confidentiality. Let them know you are there for them, with support and concern, even after the TalkSheet discussion has been completed.

Know what your goals are. A TalkSheet discussion should be more than a "bull session." TalkSheets are designed to move along toward a goal, but you need to identify that goal in advance. What would you like the young people to learn? What truth should they discover? What is the goal of the session? If you don't know where you are going, it is doubtful you will get there.

GROUND RULES FOR AN EFFECTIVE TALKSHEET DISCUSSION

It may be helpful to begin your TalkSheet discussion with a few ground rules. Keep the rules to a minimum, of course, but most of the time knowing what is expected of them will be appreciated by the students. The following are suggestions for ground rules:

• **"What is said in this room stays in this room."**
Confidentiality is vitally important if a healthy discussion is to occur. The only time it should be broken is when a student reveals he or she is going to harm himself or herself or another.

• **"No put-downs."**
Mutual respect is important. If someone disagrees with another's comment, he or she can raise his or her hand for permission to express an opinion on the *subject*, but not of the person. It is acceptable to attack ideas, but not each other.

• **"There is no such thing as a dumb question."**
Your group members must feel free to ask questions at any time. The best way to learn is to seek answers.

• **"No one is forced to talk."**
Let all members know they have the right to pass or remain silent on any question.

• **"Only one person speaks at a time."**
This is a good way to teach mutual respect. Each person's opinion is worthwhile and deserves to be heard.

If members of the group violate these rules during the discussion or engage in disruptive or negative behavior, it would be wise to stop and deal with the problem before continuing.

USING THE BIBLE WITH THE TALKSHEETS

Adults often begin discussions with young people assuming teenagers believe the Bible has authority over their lives. Adults either begin their discussions with Scripture or quickly support their contentions with Bible verses. But today's adolescents do not necessarily begin with the same assumption. They often begin with their own life situations, then decide if the Bible fits their needs. TalkSheets have been designed to begin your discussion with the realities of the adolescent world and then move toward Scripture. This give you the opportunity to show kids that the Bible can be their guide and God does have something to say to them about their own unique situations.

The last activity on each TalkSheet involves Scripture. These Bible references were selected for their relevance to each particular issue and for their potential to generate healthy discussion. They are not to be considered exhaustive. It was assumed you will feel free to add whatever other Scriptures you think pertinent. The passages listed are just the tip of the iceberg, inviting you to "search the Scriptures" and dig deeper.

After the Scriptures have been read aloud, ask your students to develop a biblical principle that can guide their lives. For example, after reading the passages on the topic of Christian service ("Going Crazy with God"), the group may summarize by saying, "The Gospel is more than simply telling others about Christ's love and forgiveness. The Lord also wants us to serve him by serving others and working toward social justice."

A WORD OF CAUTION . . .

Many of the TalkSheets in this book deal with topics that may be sensitive or considered controversial. Discussing subjects such as sexuality, rock music, satanism, partying, or the obscene may not be appreciated or understood by everyone in the church. Whenever you encourage discussion on such subjects or invite your students to express their opinions (on any subject), no matter how "off base" they may be, you risk the possibility of being criticized by parents or other concerned people in your church. They may believe you are teaching heresy or questionable values.

The best way to avoid problems is to use good judgment. If you suspect a particular TalkSheet is going to cause problems, it would be expedient to think twice before you use it. Sometimes the damage done by proceeding against your better judgment outweighs the potential good you might achieve.

In order to avoid misunderstandings, provide parents and others to whom you are accountable with copies of the TalkSheet before you use it. Inform them of the type of discussion you hope to encourage and the goal you hope to accomplish.

It is always a good idea for your students to take their TalkSheets home to discuss them with their parents. They might wish to ask their parents how they, as young people, would have answered some of the questions.

HIGH SCHOOL ADVENTURE

1

High school will be _____ than middle/junior high school.

_____ **Better**   _____ **Worse**

Why? _____

_____

_____

2

Place an **X** on the line before each of the following questions about entering high school if they are of concern to you.

_____ Will anybody like me?
_____ Will I make a sports team?
_____ Can I get along with the teachers?
_____ Will I have enough time between classes?
_____ Will I have the right clothes?
_____ Will I make the right friends?
_____ Will I be able to find my classes?
_____ Will the older students be nice to me?
_____ How tough will it be to make new friends?
_____ Are there lots of fights?
_____ Will I fit in?
_____ Will I find a boyfriend/girlfriend?
_____ Will I have enough privacy in the showers after P.E.?
_____ Will I be too big/too small?

_____ Will I get good enough grades?
_____ How hard are classes going to be?
_____ Will people make fun of my Christian beliefs?
_____ How will I know if I am taking the right classes?
_____ Will I be tempted to do drugs?
_____ Will I be harassed by a gang?
_____ Will the teachers be helpful?
_____ How much homework will I have?
_____ Will I get into much trouble?
_____ Will other kids pick on me?
_____ Will my stuff get stolen?
Write others here:

_____
_____
_____

3

How will your parents change when you get into high school? (✓ Check those that apply.)

_____ They will be more worried about my grades.
_____ They will expect more out of me.
_____ They will give me more privileges.
_____ They will worry more about me.
_____ They will be more concerned about my church involvement.
_____ They will pressure me more about sports.

_____ They will be less worried about my grades.
_____ They will expect less out of me.
_____ They will give me fewer privileges.
_____ They will worry less about me.
_____ They will be less concerned about my church involvement.
_____ They will pressure me less about sports.

4

What will your relationship with God be like when you are in high school?

_____ It will be more important than it is today.
_____ It will be about the same as it is today.
_____ It will be less important than it is today.

5

Read the following Scriptures and write out what you think each has to say about growing up.

1 Corinthians 13:11 _____

2 Timothy 2:15 _____

2 Peter 3:18 _____

HIGH SCHOOL ADVENTURE
Topic: Transitioning to High School

Purpose of this Session:

Junior highers/middle schoolers transitioning to high school are often filled with both anticipation and dread. The high school adventure often begins in a panic. Young adolescents in transition to high school often interpret change as loss. They lose relationships with teachers, friends, the old school structure, or involvement in sports and other extracurricular activities. Christian young people often are worried about how high schoolers will respond to their faith. Verbalizing their apprehensions and worries about the upcoming changes can go a long way to help kids actively cope with the transition.

To Introduce the Topic:

Tell your group you are all going to make up a story about the first day of high school. Begin by saying, "It was the first day of high school for Jason, who . . ." then have a young person add the next part of the plot. Let volunteers continue the story, but be sure they keep it clean and focused on the first day of high school. You are sure to end up with a wild but good introduction to a discussion on what high school will be like.

The Discussion:

Item #1: Begin by talking about how you would have answered this question when you were their age. Then let the young people share some of their responses to "why." Act as moderator and use effective listening. You will gain valuable insight into how they feel about the transition they are making.

Item #2: This item will help you better understand the worries and concerns of your students. Give the group members a chance to identify their top five questions. Lead the group into compiling a top ten list by group voting. Then as a group, answer the top ten questions.

Item #3: Kids in transition want freedom and security. They want to move away from their parents, but they hope their parents will still be there for them. Do not let this turn into a gripe session about parents. Rather, look at what would be reasonable changes for parents to make and why. This is an opportunity for you to empathize with kids *and* support parental authority.

Item #4: Explore how the group members feel their relationships with God may change over the next few years of high school.

Item #5: Ask the students to relate these Scriptures to making the move to high school. Encourage them to see how God is available to them as they go through the necessary changes in their lives.

To Close the Session:

Summarize what has been said during the discussion. Point out that many of the group members had similar concerns about high school. If you feel comfortable doing so, tell about your transition to high school. Wrap up by reading Psalm 20 or another psalm of trust and security in God.

Outside Activities:

1. Ask one or more Christian high school students to sit on a panel. On 3 x 5 cards, have the group members write down questions they have about high school for the panel to answer. Keep the questions anonymous to protect the group members from individual embarrassment.

2. An alternative to the panel would be for the group members to write short, open, and anonymous letters to high school students, expressing their concerns about high school. You can screen these and hand them out to high school students to write personalized responses. Code the letters so you know whom to hand them back to. It works out best if you pair males with males and females with females. Often the transitioning junior highers/middle schoolers express interest in meeting the high school students who responded to their letters.

SEX TALKS

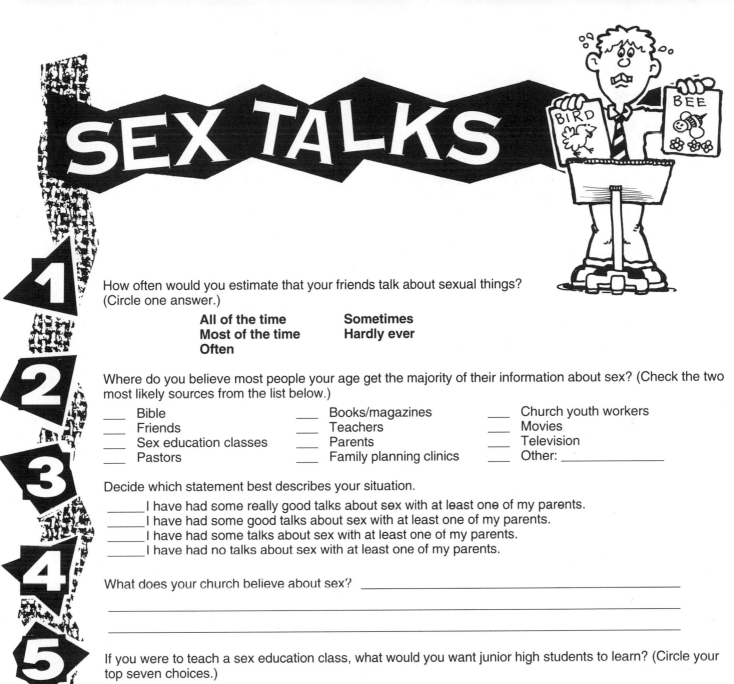

1 How often would you estimate that your friends talk about sexual things? (Circle one answer.)

All of the time   **Sometimes**
Most of the time   **Hardly ever**
Often

2 Where do you believe most people your age get the majority of their information about sex? (Check the two most likely sources from the list below.)

___ Bible   ___ Books/magazines   ___ Church youth workers
___ Friends   ___ Teachers   ___ Movies
___ Sex education classes ___ Parents   ___ Television
___ Pastors   ___ Family planning clinics ___ Other: _____

3 Decide which statement best describes your situation.

_____ I have had some really good talks about sex with at least one of my parents.
_____ I have had some good talks about sex with at least one of my parents.
_____ I have had some talks about sex with at least one of my parents.
_____ I have had no talks about sex with at least one of my parents.

4 What does your church believe about sex? _____

_____

_____

5 If you were to teach a sex education class, what would you want junior high students to learn? (Circle your top seven choices.)

a. What God has to say about sex
b. Reasons to wait until marriage
c. Sexually transmitted diseases
d. Birth control
e. What adults think about sex
f. Pregnancy stuff
g. What girls think and what boys think about sex
h. How to say no to sex
i. Bodily changes
j. The good stuff about sex

k. Relationships
l. How to have sex
m. Pornography
n. Abortion
o. Sexual abuse
p. Bodily differences between males and females
q. Homosexuality
r. Sexual morals
s. Other stuff:

_____

_____

6 Decide how the following passage applies to getting a good sex education.

Proverbs 7:1-27 _____

_____

_____

SEX TALKS
Topic: Sex Education

Purpose of this Session:

Interest in the opposite sex increases with grade level through elementary and junior high/middle school. Sex education that for all intents and purposes informs kids how to have sex is provided in most schools in America. Young teenagers are constantly bombarded with the message that premarital sex is acceptable. This TalkSheet offers the opportunity to talk with young people about the kind of sex education they have received and what they really need.

To Introduce the Topic:

Put the word *sex* on the chalkboard or on a large piece of newsprint. Ask the students to list the first things they think of when they see the word *sex*. Expect some self-conscious laughter and giggles at this point. State that you believe you can discuss sex without acting in an immature manner and without putting others down. You may want to consider separating the boys and the girls for the discussion, then bringing them together for a process time and wrap-up. While separated, the boys and the girls can think of some questions they have for the opposite sex.

The Discussion:

Item #1: Sex talk increases with grade level, paralleling interest in the opposite sex. After listening to their answers, ask the students why they believe there is more talk about sex as they have gotten older. Point out that puberty and curiosity both encourage an interest in sex. This interest is normal (not sinful) and God-given. God created the hormones in our bodies that get us thinking and wanting to talk about sex. It is not our interest in sex that is sinful, rather the decisions we make because of that interest.

Item #2: Inventory the group's three or four top choices. Ask how helpful each of the top sources has been to them. Ask them to decide which source on the list would be the most dependable. You may find it interesting to ask how helpful the sex education they have received at school has been. In all probability, they will not include parents or the church on their list. Share the need for more reliable information rather than that which comes from friends or other unqualified sources. Most of their attitudes are based on misleading information they absorb, especially from the media, without their even knowing they are doing so.

Item #3: Take time to discuss the barriers to talking with parents about sex.

Item #4: Collect all the different perceptions of what the church believes and write them down where everyone can see them. Then decide which are true and which are false.

Item #5: Use this opportunity to get in touch with what your group believes it needs to know more about. You will not have enough time to talk about each choice, but you can use this to help plan future sex education talks.

Item #6: Focusing on what God wants Christians to do sexually, ask the students to share their thoughts provoked by the passage of Scripture. Avoid being judgmental in presenting God's view. Point out that God wants the best for all of us, which is why he states that sex be reserved for the marriage commitment.

To Close the Session:

Although there is a significant minority that is involved in sexual activity, for the most part, junior high/middle school students are not engaged in premarital sex. However, the attitudes these students adopt as they move up in grade levels become more sexually permissive. They need to hear that the Bible, God, and Christians they trust want them to know the truth about sex. Point out that God wants the best for their lives and the best includes waiting until marriage to have sex. Encourage them to seek out God's perspective on sex before they make a decision they may regret.

Outside Activity:

Suggest they write anonymous "Dear Abby" type letters concerning any questions they may have about sexual matters. Answer the questions the following week.

TOGETHER

The best age for a boy or a girl to go with someone is . . . (Circle one age.)

Best age for girls: 10 11 12 13 14 15 16
Best age for boys: 10 11 12 13 14 15 16

How much pressure is there at your school to be together with a member of the opposite sex?

_____**Big-time pressure**
_____**Some pressure**
_____**A little pressure**
_____**No pressure**

YES, NO, or **MAYBE SO.** Write in your answer.

a. ___Most people my age have already been in a close relationship with a member of the opposite sex.
b. ___One must be in a relationship with the opposite sex to be popular.
c. ___The more attractive a young person is, the better the opposite sex relationship she or he will have.
d. ___In junior high/middle school, girls and boys should be friends, but not boyfriend/girlfriend.
e. ___A relationship with someone of the opposite sex can help you grow as a Christian.
f. ___A young person's parents should approve of any relationship he or she has with the opposite sex.
g. ___Girls are too pushy in relationships with boys.
h. ___You should know someone a long time before going out/being with them.

Place an **A** next to those things you consider an **advantage** to being together with someone of the opposite sex. Place a **D** next to those things you see as a **disadvantage** to being together.

_____You get to talk on the phone a lot.
_____You have to worry about what your parents will say.
_____You could end up doing sexual things.
_____You can't spend as much time with your friends.
_____You could spend lots of time with one person.

_____You might be more popular.
_____You could have fun.
_____You could waste time.
_____You might break up.
_____You have to hide where you are going.

Read the following verses and summarize how they relate to young people going together.

1 Kings 11:1-4 _____

Romans 12:9-11 _____

1 Corinthians 10:23-24 _____

TOGETHER
Topic: Going Together/Pseudo-dating

Purpose of this Session:

Not all young people in junior high/middle school have a relationship with the opposite sex. In fact, most do not. But the pressure is intense at many schools for the kids to pair off. If this is a pressure your kids face, this TalkSheet can provide a valuable opportunity to dialogue with your students about the tension they face. You may want to consider separating the boys and the girls for the TalkSheet discussion, then bringing them together for a process time and wrap-up. While separated, the boys and the girls can think of some questions they have for the opposite sex. See also "OPPOSITE SEX BLUES," page 80 and "SEX IS NOT A FOUR-LETTER WORD," page 76.

To Introduce the Topic:

Ask the group to create a list of all the things students who are going together do while they are together. The list could include such things as talk on the phone, go to the mall together, hang out in dark places to kiss, go out with a group of friends, go to the movies, or hang out at school. See how big a list you can generate in a given time period.

Another good way to introduce this subject is through the production of original skits. Separate the young people into groups of three to six and have them prepare an original skit on junior high/middle school romance. Suggest only titles, such as "Junior High Love," "First Love," or "Hanging Out Together." Make sure the groups keep the skits clean and that they stick with the theme of junior high/middle school romance.

The Discussion:

Item #1: Take this chance to define terms since in different places young people use different terms. What used to be called "going steady" is now called "going out," "going together," or "being together." Ask the students to justify the ages they chose. Usually young people see no problem with going together at a young age.

Item #2: Support those young people who are not going or who have not gone with someone. Unfortunately, curiosity and peer pressure often kick in before the hormones to force kids into premature relationships.

Item #3: You will find it easy to create a debate with these statements. Explore with the group why going together is so important and what happens when you do not participate in the pseudo-dating ritual.

Item #4: Here you have an opportunity to explore the inherent dangers in premature relationships with the opposite sex as well as the up side of these relationships. Both aspects need to be explored.

Item #5: Ask several people to share how they felt the Scriptures related to going together.

To Close the Session:

This issue is a tough one because it is controversial. Many adults believe young people are growing up too fast when they go together so young. They point to evidence that suggests the younger one is involved in opposite sex dating and pseudo-dating relationships, the younger one is engaged in premarital sex. Going together at this age also trivializes the importance of relationships. But other adults see going together as a positive life-skills course in relationships. In wrapping up the talk, it is important that you keep this balanced perspective in mind. Kids not wanting to participate in going together need to be affirmed and supported. Kids also need to be aware of the dangers of going together at such a young age. However, if you present this in a judgmental tone, the young people will turn you off and your efforts will be counterproductive.

Outside Activity:

Promote group togetherness rather than individual pairing off by asking the group to plan a group date.

BIBLE DOCTRINESZZZZZ

Circle each of the following that you believe are Bible doctrines.

Anarchy	**Hedonism**	**Justification**	**Predestination**
Atonement	**Imputation**	**Materialism**	**Regeneration**
Baptism	**Incarnation**	**Pantheism**	**Salvation**
Darwinism	**Islam**	**Pessimism**	**Stewardship**

Put a question mark (?) on the line before each of the doctrines listed below that you know little or nothing about.

The doctrine of . . .

___ Redemption	___ Creation
___ Trinity	___ Sin
___ The Second Coming	___ Grace
___ Demons	___ The church
___ The Bible's inspiration	___ Resurrection

Your opinion, please.   **! = THAT'S RIGHT   ? = MAYBE   X = NO WAY**

_____ **a.** What you believe about God and the Bible makes a difference in the way you live your life.
_____ **b.** Young people are not smart enough to understand Bible doctrines.
_____ **c.** Bible doctrines can help people with their problems.
_____ **d.** Learning the different Bible doctrines makes you a Christian.
_____ **e.** Knowing Bible doctrines will keep you from being deceived into believing something that is not true.

Read the following Scriptures and write what you think each has to say about Bible doctrines.

Ephesians 4:14 _____

_____

1 Timothy 4:16 _____

_____

Titus 1:9 _____

_____

BIBLE DOCTRINESZZZZZ

Topic: Bible Doctrines

Purpose of this Session:

Since young people have so many concerns and problems, time is often devoted to topical studies similar to those found in this book. But relatively little time is spent on the major doctrines developed throughout the Bible and identified by the church fathers as important. This TalkSheet examines the importance of Bible doctrines and helps your group identify the ones it wishes to study.

To Introduce the Topic:

Bring a bottle of sunscreen to the group. Ask the kids what can happen during the summer when you do not apply sunscreen at the beach or the pool—you can get sunburned. But if you apply this sunscreen, you are protected from the sun. The Bible is like sunscreen because it can protect us from the false beliefs and teachings that lead us astray. Many Bible teachings have been organized into themes or subject groupings about God and his kingdom.

The Discussion:

Item #1: The following are the Bible doctrines: atonement, baptism, imputation, incarnation, justification, predestination, regeneration, salvation, and stewardship.

Item #2: Take a closer look at the Bible doctrines found in Items #1 and #2 by using a Bible dictionary, and look up the terms that are not Bible doctrines.

Item #3: Focus on how Bible doctrines can help you live your life. Point out that what you believe affects how you live your life. For example, if a person believes there is no heaven or hell, he or she will live differently than someone who firmly believes heaven and hell exist.

Item #4: See if your group can come up with one statement about Bible doctrine based upon the three passages. Example: Sound doctrine will help you live the Christian life.

To Close the Session:

Go back to the introductory activity. Tell the group that you cannot put sunscreen on only once in a lifetime. It must be applied over and over again if you want protection from the sun. The study of the Bible and Bible doctrines is like sunscreen. It protects you, but it must be studied again and again.

Outside Activity:

Take the doctrines identified in Item #2 and spend additional time studying these as a group. You could ask the pastor to attend the group to define some of the Bible doctrines, answer questions about them, and teach the kids how they can use study tools like Bible dictionaries to study doctrines.

GOING CRAZY WITH GOD

Estimate how much time each week you spend helping others who are not members of your family. (Circle one.)

No time
About one to two hours
Three to four hours
Five or more hours

What do you like most about the following want ad? _____

_____

What do you like least about the ad? _____

_____

VOLUNTEERS DESPERATELY NEEDED: We want young people who desire to help those in need. Jobs available in a wide variety of areas. No minimum age requirement. Eternal rewards. No experience needed. Your participation is critical. Apply today! Call 1-800-555-MINISTRY.

I would like to participate in a Christian service project . . . (Circle one.)

a. that only takes a little bit of time and work.
b. that takes some time and work every month.
c. that takes some time and work every week.
d. forget about it; count me out; no way; I don't want to get involved.

Underline the one that you would most like to volunteer to do.

a. Read the Bible and Christian books to blind senior adults living in rest homes.
b. Collect warm clothing for the homeless.
c. Raise money to build a playground for an inner-city church day-care center.
d. Take sack lunches to homeless families.
e. Talk with AIDS patients who are dying in the hospital.
f. Prepare food in a rescue mission or Salvation Army kitchen.
g. Organize a party for kids living in a children's home/orphanage.
h. Volunteer to help with Special Olympics.
i. Visit kids with cancer who are hospitalized.

Decide which of the following Scriptures are examples of Christian service and which are examples of selfishness.

Haggai 1:5, 6	**Genesis 50:21**	**Psalm 109:16**	**Matthew 19:21**	**Matthew 25:41-43**
John 13:4, 5	**Luke 10:30-32**	**Acts 9:36**	**Acts 5:1, 2**	**1 Corinthians 10:33**

Date Used: _____   Group: _____

GOING CRAZY WITH GOD
Topic: Christian Service

Purpose of this Session:

When people think of junior high/middle school ministry, they normally think of parties, discipline problems, or baby-sitting. What they do not often consider is Christian service. Yet young teenagers are ripe for doing some kind of Christian social action. Use this TalkSheet to explore this life-changing topic. Maybe your group will decide to "go crazy with God."

To Introduce the Topic:

Create a short quiz, specific to your area, that tests your group's knowledge of local community services. The following is an example of such a quiz:

1. Where would an adult woman and her children go if she were the victim of domestic violence?
2. Where would a 15-year-old girl go who was experiencing a crisis pregnancy?
3. If a mentally retarded teenager were looking for a job, where would she or he go for help?
4. What agency would a young mother with a developmentally disabled preschool child turn to for help?
5. Where would a family of five turn for emergency financial assistance?
6. What is the name of our local children's home or orphanage?
7. Name a hospital in our area with a special unit for children with cancer.

Give the quiz to your group, along with several information and referral books to be used as references. Break into smaller groups and see who can complete the quiz the fastest with the most correct answers. Award a prize that can be shared with everyone.

An additional introductory activity using newspapers can also be effectively used as a lead-in. Divide the students into small groups. Distribute newspapers to the groups and explain that they are to find example articles of where Christ's Gospel is working, as well as examples of where the Gospel is needed.

The Discussion:

Item #1: Like adults, kids can tend to fudge in favor of making themselves look good. Ask the kids to give examples of how they help others, as well as ways they ignore the needs of others.

Item #2: Let the young people share the pros and cons of volunteering to serve others. Explore ways the negative aspects of service to others can be overcome.

Item #3: Get a group consensus regarding the kids' willingness and desire to serve. This item should give you a group commitment level if you take the average of the young people's responses.

Item #4: In addition to the activity ideas listed, see how big a list your group can generate. Write the list on the chalkboard or on newsprint.

Item #5: Have the young people report their findings on these verses. Ask them to relate what they learned about Christian service from looking at both sets of passages.

To Close the Session:

The Gospel is more than an individual proclaiming repentance and belief in the risen Savior who can forgive sin. The Gospel has a social dimension. The concept of the social Gospel prominent in much of mainline Protestantism in America was based on the nineteenth-century Great Awakening. Christians desired to proclaim the love of Christ through their actions. They saw how sin had manifested itself through economic injustice. They sought to stand up for Christ and say no to sin by fighting oppression. Explain to the group that the Christian life is an adventure that is more than a personal transformation. As Tony Campolo points out, Christ is also the transformer of society. Sin affects more than just individuals—it permeates all of society. And Christians are called to work for the good of mankind (Titus 2:7, 3:8). You can close by reading Matthew 25:31-46.

Outside Activities:

1. There are many great ideas for service projects in the book *Ideas for Social Action* by Anthony Campolo (Youth Specialties/Zondervan, 1983).
2. Choose a need identified in the introduction activity and take this on as a group project.

AN X-RATED WORLD

PARENTAL WARNING: THIS TALKSHEET CONTAINS OBJECTIONABLE MATERIAL

1 How did you react when you first saw the parental advisory warning shown on the right? (Circle one.)

a. I scanned the TalkSheet to find the objectionable material.
b. I did not notice it.
c. I ignored it.

2 How common are the following in your life?

R = RARE   F = FREQUENT   E = EVERYDAY

__ Hear four-letter words.
__ Listen to music with sex themes.
__ Use four-letter words.
__ Look at a sexual picture in a magazine.
__ Hear someone talk about pornography.

__ Watch R-rated movies.
__ Hear dirty jokes.
__ Laugh at profanity.
__ View questionable TV.

3 What do you think?

	AGREE	DISAGREE
a. One has to use four-letter words to be popular.	___	___
b. One should not watch movies that contain profanity.	___	___
c. Christians should be angry about the obscene things in our world.	___	___
d. Dirty jokes are harmless fun.	___	___
e. It's impossible to not use four-letter words at my school.	___	___
f. Television is growing more obscene.	___	___
g. Listening to rock music with sexually explicit lyrics hurts one's morals.	___	___

4 How would you respond if you were in each of the following situations?

a. On the way to school, the kids you are with begin listening to a cassette of music that is dirty.

_____

b. Flipping through the cable channels on TV at a sleepover, your friend stops at a stand-up comedian who is really vulgar.

_____

c. You and two friends are at a record/video store looking at the posters. Your two friends are giggling and staring at a poster of an almost naked person.

_____

d. A dirty joke book is being passed around your classroom at school. The book is passed to you.

_____

5 Read **Philippians 4:8, 9** and write what you think it has to say about living in an X-rated world.

_____

_____

AN X-RATED WORLD
Topic: The Obscene and Pop Culture

Purpose of this Session:

There was a time in the not-so-distant past that society strongly believed young teenagers needed to be protected from the obscene in culture. At that time, the obscene existed only on the fringes of pop culture. Times have changed. Today, kids have relatively easy access to the obscene because the obscene has become mainstream. Today's pop culture is crude and lewd and growing more profane with each new TV season or stand-up comic. Constant exposure to the obscene in our world is having a numbing effect on young teens. What shocks parents of young teens does little to arouse a sense of outrage in the kids. This TalkSheet gives you the opportunity to talk with your kids about the effects the obscene is having in their lives.

To Introduce the Topic:

On newsprint or on a chalkboard large enough for everyone in your group to see, write the following seven words: *obscene, vulgar, lewd, dirty, pornographic, filthy,* and *lascivious.* Ask the students to tell you what they think when they see these words. You will get a variety of responses ranging from sex to sin. Discuss with the group what the word *obscene* means. Most kids think it means sex or cursing. Give them a broader definition. Remember to point out that *sex* and *obscene* are not the same. Read a dictionary definition of *obscene. Webster's New World Dictionary* defines it as "offensive to modesty or decency; lewd." Tell the group members that the discussion they are about to have will be about the obscene in their world and how Christians can respond to it. Ask them for examples of the obscene in your community. Answers can range from the wearing of T-shirts with sexually explicit messages to TV programming.

   If you are getting a lot of giggling, laughing, and teasing, challenge the group to act like adults and have a mature discussion of this important topic.

The Discussion:

Item #1: Many of the young people, if they are honest, will pick "a." Take a minute and discuss why people are attracted to objectionable material. Point out that the more available objectionable material is, the more likely people will read it, watch it, and listen to it.

Item #2: This activity will give you an idea of how your group of young teens has been influenced by the culture that surrounds them. Avoid being judgmental here. Let kids share their responses. Let them talk about how difficult it is to live the Christian life in an obscene world.

Item #3: Open each of these statements to debate. Normally you will get a wide variety of opinions. See if your students can decide how the obscene has an impact on their everyday lives. Take a moment and talk about why the world in which they live has become so much more obscene. Ask them to compare the world their grandparents grew up in with the world in which they must grow up.

Item #4: These mini-tension getters make great role-play situations as well as discussion starters on how to handle everyday situations involving the obscene. Ask the kids to share "tension getters" that they have faced. The group can brainstorm Christian responses to these difficult but real dilemmas.

Item #5: Discuss with the group how this verse can help a Christian evaluate the world in which she or he lives. Ask the students how they could use this verse in their own lives.

To Close the Session:

Ask the group to imagine the average young teenager. Describe some of the attitudes and behaviors of this average young teenager as she or he goes through the junior high and high school years. Mention things that your kids have brought up during your discussion (things like viewing R-rated movies, reading a dirty joke book, attending a vulgar rock concert, believing people are sex objects, or thinking cursing is something one has to do). Now ask the group to predict the kind of life this mythical person might have. What kind of relationship with God might he or she have? What kind of parent might he or she be? What kind of values might he or she adopt? How will this person learn to treat others?

   Close by telling the group that society is getting more worldly. They can be like the world or they can rise above the world. And only they can choose!

Outside Activity:

Ask the group to give examples of each of the following:
1. An obscene movie   2. An obscene comedian   3. An obscene rock band   4. An obscene television program
   Now ask the students to interview their parents and ask them to give examples of the obscene for the same four pop entertainment choices. At the next group meeting, you can discuss how much more obscene our culture has become and what a Christian response would be to the moral decline.

THE LEAST OF THESE

1 Homelessness is . . . (✓ Check one.)

_____ **increasing.**
_____ **remaining the same.**
_____ **decreasing.**

2 If you were to talk with a homeless person, how do you think you would feel? (You can circle more than one.)

Afraid	**Sad**	**Thankful**	**Superior**
Strange	**Disgusted**	**Helpless**	**Confused**
Mad	**Offended**	**Sympathetic**	**Judgmental**
Joyful	**Who cares?**	**Glad**	**Hesitant**

3 Homeless people are lazy.

_____ **True** _____ **False**

4 Your opinion, please. **YES, NO,** or **MAYBE SO.**

	YES	NO	MAYBE
a. There are homeless people in our community.	____	____	____
b. There are homeless young people my age in our community.	____	____	____
c. Most people do not care about the homeless.	____	____	____
d. There is nothing that I can do to help the homeless.	____	____	____
e. If Christians don't help the homeless, no one will.	____	____	____
f. Churches could do more to help the homeless.	____	____	____

5 Claudia took her place in the cafeteria line. Then she noticed she was in line beside Tony—the geekiest boy in school! All her friends called him "homeless." His clothes were never clean and they looked like he picked them out of the garbage. No one knew much about him. I guess it was because no one really cared. Just then Tony turned toward Claudia and smiled. "Oh no!" she thought. "Now what? Everyone is watching me to see what I will do."

Why do you think kids make fun of Tony? _____

_____

What would you do if you were Claudia? _____

_____

6 Read the following verses found in the book of Proverbs and summarize them in five words or less.

Proverbs 14:21 _____

Proverbs 14:31 _____

Proverbs 29:7 _____

Proverbs 31:9 _____

THE LEAST OF THESE
Topic: The Homeless

Purpose of this Session:

Junior high/middle schoolers are well aware of the problem of homelessness. They see people aimlessly walking the streets, the "will work for food" signs, and reports of the problem on the evening news. Homelessness is a visible problem in the United States and other parts of the world. The problem may be visible, yet it is quite misunderstood. Use this TalkSheet to help clear up some of the misconceptions about the issue and to challenge young people to become part of the solution in the name of Jesus.

To Introduce the Topic:

Divide the young people into small groups and tell them they are advertising agencies assigned to create a 30-second public service commercial about the homeless, that will be on national television during prime time. They need to spotlight the problem of homelessness for TV viewers. Allow enough time for them to make up their skits before they present them to each other.

An alternative would be to have someone unknown to the group impersonate a homeless person; someone who is up-to-date and concerned about the problem to speak to the group. She or he can give a short talk on the problems a homeless family has—food, shelter, medical care, spiritual problems, life-threatening problems, and so on.

The Discussion:

Item #1: Get the young people's perceptions of the size of the problem of homelessness by asking them to report their answers.

Item #2: Ask how many of the kids have ever talked with a homeless person. Let the group share the different feelings it has regarding the homeless.

Item #3: This activity hits at a myth about the homeless. Most homeless people are not lazy. There are unfortunate situations like unemployment, chronic mental illness, alcoholism, drug addiction, AIDS, single parenting, and difficult physical disabilities that contribute to the homelessness problem. In the past there was the notion of the deserving poor and those who did not deserve help. The idea persists today that some individuals are down on their luck and deserve help or are very disabled and society has a moral obligation to care for them. Ask your group what it thinks about this idea and what Christ might think about it. What responsibility do Christians have concerning this enormous social problem?

Item #4: Let the group members share their responses to these statements. Allow the group to debate the more controversial issues.

Item #5: This "tension getter" can be used to talk about the compassion of Christ that others in unfortunate situations need. Let different group members answer the questions.

Item #6: Have the group summarize these passages and ask for examples of how the verses could be applied to today's problem of homelessness.

To Close the Session:

Point out that the problem of homelessness arises from a multitude of conditions existing in our society. Some are homeless because of alcoholism, drug addiction, unemployment, chronic mental illness, physical disabilities, AIDS, domestic violence, single-parent families, and government policies on welfare and affordable housing, to name just some of the major contributing factors. Some of these homeless do not want help—they prefer their chosen lifestyle. But most of the homeless want help desperately. Government assistance and homeless shelters are not near enough. Emphasize that many homeless need much more than just shelter. Christ waits for his people to touch the lives of the homeless in his name.

Outside Activities:

1. Ask the group to create a gratitude list—all the things for which the students can be thankful. The list could include the simplest things that we take for granted, like taking a shower.

2. Create a task force of young people willing to investigate the problem of homelessness in your community. The task force can report back with recommendations as to what the youth group can do to take the love of Christ into the community.

READY, SET, GROW

1 Growing as a Christian means a person has to give up having fun.

_____ **Yes** _____ **No** _____ **I don't know**

2 Christians should want to grow as Christians to . . . (Choose the one best reason from the list below.)

___ avoid going to hell.
___ better confront life's problems.
___ be more like Jesus.

___ have a better relationship with God.
___ be protected from sin.
___ be a role model for others.

3 In order to grow as a Christian, you should . . . (Check those you believe are necessary to grow as a Christian.)

___ tell others about Christ.
___ never ever sin again.
___ be confirmed.
___ get baptized.
___ willingly help others.
___ memorize Bible verses.
___ feel guilty a lot of the time.
___ admit your sins.
___ be with Christians your age.
___ go to youth group.
___ talk with other Christian adults about how they have become more like Jesus.

___ read the Bible on a regular basis.
___ learn about Bible doctrines.
___ pray.
___ become a member of a church.
___ tithe money to the church.
___ read Christian books and magazines.
___ worship God.
___ believe in Jesus Christ.
___ live what you believe.
___ Other: _____

4 What do you think?

		THAT'S ME	THAT'S NOT ME
a.	I have spent time trying to understand my Christian faith.	____	____
b.	I pray in other places besides church.	____	____
c.	I have talked with another Christian about my questions regarding Christianity.	____	____
d.	When I have a problem, I consider how Jesus might want me to handle it.	____	____
e.	I read my Bible in places other than church.	____	____
f.	I have talked with my friends about what it means to be a Christian.	____	____
g.	I am regularly involved in my church's activities.	____	____
h.	I have helped someone in need during the past month.	____	____
i.	When I have a life decision to make, I talk it over with God.	____	____
j.	Christianity is one of the most important influences in my life.	____	____
k.	I have experienced God's love and forgiveness.	____	____
l.	I realize I need God's continual grace and love.	____	____
m.	I attend church more than once a week.	____	____

5 Complete the following sentence: **One thing I need to do more of to grow as a Christian is . . .**

_____

6 Read each of the following passages of Scripture and write out what you believe is the common theme.

Luke 2:52 **Ephesians 4:14, 15** **1 Peter 2:2** **2 Peter 3:18**

_____

READY, SET, GROW
Topic: Christian Growth

Purpose of this Session:

Young teens are capable of becoming like Jesus, and Christ-likeness is what Christian growth is all about. For too long the church has neglected this age group's Christian growth needs, focusing on Bible memory and quiz teams. Use this TalkSheet as an evaluation tool to examine how well you are meeting the needs of your group as well as an opportunity for Christian growth.

To Introduce the Topic:

For this introduction you will need to gather a variety of toys for different age levels. The following are examples of these:

BABIES	ELEMENTARY AGE	ADULTS
Rattle	Barbie/G.I.*Joe	Chess
Doll	Roller skates	Tennis racket
Blocks	Soccer ball	Golf club

Place these items at random on a table. If you do not have access to the items, you can write the names of each on 3 x 5 cards or sheets of paper. Tell the kids that these items are appropriate for three different age groups—babies, elementary age, and adults. Have them suggest the age group for which the items are appropriate and ask them to give reasons for their decisions. You might get the following answers: "Because blocks are boring" or "A baby could get hurt with that." Explain to your group that just as we outgrow the toys we play with, we also mature in our spiritual lives. Then pass out the TalkSheets.

The Discussion:

Item #1: "Boring Christianity" is one of the myths that adults seem to pass on to the younger generation. But Christian growth is fun. Ask the kids how you could truly grow more like Jesus without having fun. It is impossible! Talk about how our faith liberates us rather than restricts us. That is what Jesus came to do. The religious leaders of the day wanted to restrict people. God came to set us free.

Item #2: A case can be made for each of these. Ultimately, we want to be more like Jesus.

Item #3: Debate which of these is essential for Christian growth. Talk especially about how teenagers and adults together can grow in Christ. This is why we have youth group and worship.

Item #4: Ask kids to share their progress in spiritual growth. Encourage group members to be honest and supportive and to fight the urge to say what they think everyone wants to hear.

Item #5: Ask for volunteers to publicly commit. Do not force anyone.

Item #6: Examine each passage and together arrive at a common theme.

To Close the Session:

When we talk about Christian growth, we typically focus upon individual responsibility for becoming more like Jesus. But we also grow in Christ through community, which is one reason for the establishment of the church. The context for our growth is the living body of Christ, with Christ as the head. Take time to close the session by examining with the young people how the church can better promote its Christian growth.

Outside Activity:

Ask the young people to bring in to the group something that represents spiritual growth to them. It might be a certificate of baptism or a devotional guide. Perhaps a student would want to bring a worn-out pair of shoes to represent how far he has come in his spiritual journey. Another group member may want to bring her prayer journal. Let the young people share what they brought with the rest of the group.

HERE WE WAR AGAIN

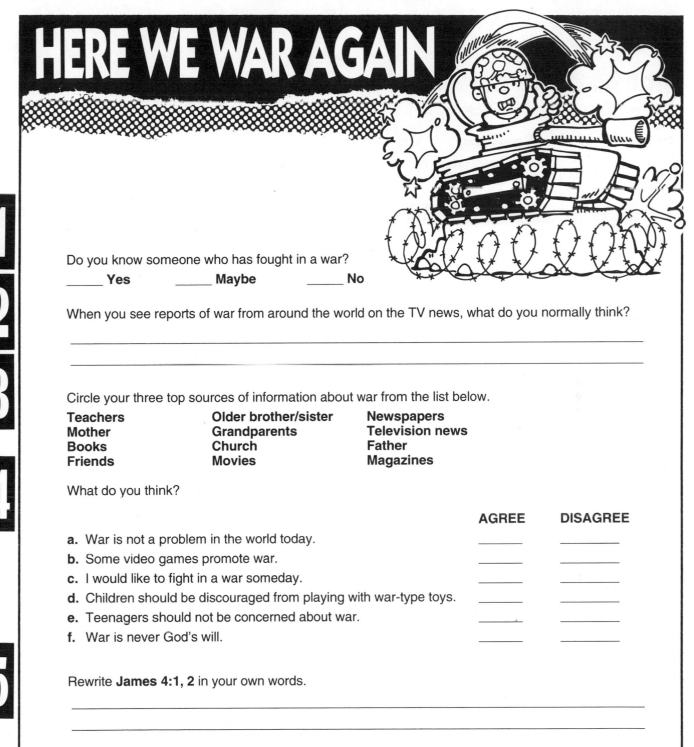

1

Do you know someone who has fought in a war?

_____ **Yes**   _____ **Maybe**   _____ **No**

2

When you see reports of war from around the world on the TV news, what do you normally think?

_____

_____

3

Circle your three top sources of information about war from the list below.

Teachers	**Older brother/sister**	**Newspapers**
Mother	**Grandparents**	**Television news**
Books	**Church**	**Father**
Friends	**Movies**	**Magazines**

4

What do you think?

	AGREE	DISAGREE
a. War is not a problem in the world today.	_____	_____
b. Some video games promote war.	_____	_____
c. I would like to fight in a war someday.	_____	_____
d. Children should be discouraged from playing with war-type toys.	_____	_____
e. Teenagers should not be concerned about war.	_____	_____
f. War is never God's will.	_____	_____

5

Rewrite **James 4:1, 2** in your own words.

_____

_____

HERE WE WAR AGAIN
Topic: Conventional War

Purpose of this Session:

Early adolescents play war games, watch war movies, hear war stories, and generally have a favorable and glorified picture of war. But war is about death and destruction, evil and pain, plunder and starvation, tragedy and tears. To quote General William Tecumseh Sherman of Civil War fame, "War is hell." General Sherman was outspoken in his belief that war must be ruthless for victory to be guaranteed. This TalkSheet gives your kids the chance to examine a fresh, biblical view of war.

To Introduce the Topic:

Break the students into small groups. Give each group paper and something to write with. Tell the kids this is a contest to write down as many movie titles as they can about a subject. At a signal tell the students they have one minute to write down as many war movie titles as possible. Give the winning group a prize like toy squirt guns. Tell them you are going to have a TalkSheet discussion on the topic of conventional war. An additional TalkSheet covering the topic of nuclear war can be found on page 41.

The Discussion:

Item #1: Let the young people share their stories of war. Ask them why they think war is usually glamorized when stories are told, books are written, and movies are made.

Item #2: Create a master list of the group's responses. Circle those responses that are common within the group. Ask the group why these responses appeared more frequently.

Item #3: Children usually report hearing the most about war from the mass media. Unfortunately, this is probably the worst place for them to get the majority of their information on such a topic. The media offer no chance for debate and dialogue nor do they offer emotional support, caring, and hope. Young people need opportunities to talk about war with adults. Adults all too frequently neglect talking about this issue even in the midst of war.

Item #4: Poll the young people on each statement. Leave room for debate on those issues where the group is not in agreement. Ask those responding to give reasons for their answers.

Item #5: Ask different young people to share what they wrote. Create a master list of all the ideas learned from the passage.

To Close the Session:

Young people need to know that Christ is the Prince of Peace. He has called each of us to be peacemakers. Unfortunately, there is evil in the world and sometimes evil necessitates war. Fortunately, God is still on the throne and in control of what happens in today's world. Christians can find hope in Christ as we spread the Gospel that includes peace throughout the world. And we can begin right here where we live. That may mean being a peacemaker on the school bus or in the cafeteria. Emphasize that each of us can work for peace.

Outside Activity:

Turn the slogan "Wage War" around into "Wage Peace." Divide the original group into smaller groups and assign them the task of identifying strategies for waging peace. Material can be researched at a local library. Together, the groups can compare their strategies and vote on one or two for action.

YOU GOTTA HAVE FAITH

1 Faith is believing something that you know is not true.

___ **I agree**.
___ **I disagree**.

2 **TRUE** or **FALSE**?

T F   It does not take much faith to believe there is a God.
T F   I am not really sure what I believe about God.
T F   Doubting God hurts one's faith.
T F   It would be easier to trust in Christ if there was more evidence that he is real.

3 Check (✓) three of the following reasons why you feel many Christian young people do not take their Christian faith seriously.

___ Living the Christian life is not worth it.
___ Christianity may not be true.
___ Christianity does not work in everyday life.
___ The Christian life is too difficult to live.
___ I don't see the importance of God in everyday living.
___ I don't see the fun in Christianity.
___ I'm too busy with other things.
___ Christianity does not make much sense.
___ The Christian life is boring.
___ Christianity is too confusing.
___ Christianity is for old people who are about to die.
___ Give your opinion: _____

4 If you took a test that showed how seriously you lived out your faith in Jesus Christ, what grade do you think you would receive? (Circle only one grade.)

A   B   C   D   F

5 After reading the following Scriptures, decide what message God wants to give you about faith.

John 20:24-29   Romans 3:22   Romans 10:17
Hebrews 11:1   Hebrews 11:6

YOU GOTTA HAVE FAITH
Topic: Faith

Purpose of this Session:

When young people think of faith, they may think of a church building or a worship service. Some think of reading the Bible or believing in religion. What do your kids think? Use this TalkSheet to explore the faith of your group of young people.

To Introduce the Topic:

Write the following headlines on the chalkboard or on newsprint. Then ask the students to say which ones they would have faith in and which ones they would not have faith in.

1. "WOMAN WITH TWO HEADS GIVES BIRTH TO TWINS"
2. "UFO CRASHES AT BOTTOM OF GRAND CANYON"
3. "YOUNG CHILD HEALED OF CANCER AFTER CHURCH PRAYS"
4. "ELVIS APPEARS AT DRUG TREATMENT CENTER IN CALIFORNIA"
5. "RAMPAGING GUERRILLA KILLS FIVE PEOPLE"
6. "MELT AWAY 100 LBS. IN A WEEK WITH SECRET DIET OF THE ASTRONAUTS"
7. "THE INCREDIBLE STORY OF A ROCK STAR JUNKIE"

   Explore the reasoning for those that are believable and those that are not. Point out the crazy faith people must have to believe some of the tabloid headlines seen in the supermarket checkout lines. Then announce the topic and pass out the TalkSheets.

The Discussion:

Item #1: Ask why many view faith as a crazy belief in something that is not true, but they believe in it anyway. Then talk about what the group is putting its faith into—the church, a set of beliefs found in a book, a quest for the meaning of life, or an historical Jesus who is who he says he is.

Item #2: Give young people the opportunity to ask questions and express their doubts. Question asking is one of the best ways to grow your faith. Be sure that your group provides a safe environment. Remind the group that there is no such thing as a dumb question.

Item #3: Let the group members share their opinions. See if the group can reach a consensus on the top three reasons. Ask the group how these three can be overcome.

Item #4: Kids can reflect on their personal faith in Jesus Christ. The young people can also grade themselves as to how well they live out their faith as a youth group.

Item #5: Have several volunteers share the message they feel God wants to give the group about faith. Take time to examine a number of the passages as a group.

To Close the Session:

Explain to the group that many people talk about faith in terms of "believing that." They believe that there is a God or that you should go to church. But is "believing that" faith the kind of faith God wants? There is nothing wrong with "believing that" faith, which focuses on information. The Bible says even the demons believe (James 2:19). But there is another kind of faith, a "believing in" faith. This kind of faith agrees with God. It is based upon facts like "believing that" faith, but it runs deeper. It is a relationship faith that focuses on the person of God and his love. It is a relationship faith. "Believing in" faith is based upon sound historical, factual information. God did not expect us to walk around lost and in the dark. The Bible provides us with the facts of our faith but we still must have that "believe in" faith to have a personal relationship with Jesus Christ.

Outside Activity:

Have the young people each make a collage that describes faith. Ask them to bring their collages to the youth group to share them. Keep them to share with parents and church members.

IS YOUR CHRISTIANITY COLOR-BLIND?

 1 When I think of being friends with someone of another race, I . . . (Circle those that apply to you.)

    a. feel very uncomfortable.

    b. know that my mom or my dad would be unhappy about it.

    c. have never really thought about it.

    d. disagree with it.

    e. think it is cool.

2 Have you ever . . .

___ heard a joke that was racist?

___ felt you might be prejudiced?

___ heard about a racially motivated fight at your school?

___ participated in racial name-calling?

___ talked with a member of another race about Jesus Christ?

3 **YES**, **NO**, or **MAYBE SO**. (Write in your answer.)

a. ___Whites owe blacks and other minorities because of past discrimination and injustice toward them.

b. ___Whites are afraid of minorities.

c. ___Minorities are as racist as whites.

d. ___There is more racism directed toward blacks than other minorities.

e. ___Minorities should quit blaming their problems on whites and do something to help themselves.

f. ___Minorities must work harder to get along with whites than whites must work to get along with minorities.

 4 Complete the following sentence: **One thing a Christian could do to fight racism is . . .**

_____

_____

_____

 5 After reading the following Scriptures, decide what message God wants to give you about racism.

    Genesis 1:27   **Luke 24:47**   **Acts 10:28**

    Romans 8:1-3   **Romans 10:12, 13**   **James 2:8, 9**

_____

_____

_____

IS YOUR CHRISTIANITY COLOR-BLIND?
Topic: Racism

Purpose of this Session:

By early adolescence, young people are well aware of race relations. Many kids will have observed numerous examples of prejudice and bigotry, even though most of them will say they are not prejudiced themselves. But racism is a persistent problem and this TalkSheet can help your group examine this important issue. Christians can reject racism and call others to treat people with the dignity and respect they deserve as creations of God.

To Introduce the Topic:

Break the students into small groups. Ask each group to build a stereotype. Let the group members decide what group of people they wish to stereotype. It could be a peer group from school like the headbangers, the bops, the stoners, or whatever groups exist in your community. It could be a race or an age group like senior citizens. Have the groups share their stereotypes, then ask them why the stereotypes persist. Are the stereotypes true? Do they help or hurt those being stereotyped? Do the stereotypes help you better understand a group of people?

The Discussion:

Item #1: Many youths have not had much personal contact with other races. The more personal and positive contact one has with other races, the less racism persists. Ask the students to share why they may (or may not) feel uncomfortable in close relationships with other races.

Item #2: Let several individuals share their experiences, then ask the group why it feels people are racist. Brainstorm what young people can do when they experience racist situations like hearing a racist joke. You can role-play different responses Christian kids could have to the situations.

Item #3: Ask for opinions on each of these statements, one at a time. These are emotional issues, so don't allow kids to put others down with their responses. Ask the young people to back up their responses with support from the Bible. This will be difficult for the kids since many of them have not considered what the Bible says about race relations.

Item #4: Give the students opportunities to explore how the church could combat the problem.

Item #5: Discuss why racism exists, especially among Christians, if God created all of us in his image and made his salvation available to all who want it.

To Close the Session:

Scripture makes it clear that God is opposed to racism in whatever form it takes. Unfortunately, the American church has a mixed record in standing against the sin of racism. This does not, however, discount what God says about racism. In the Old Testament, God taught the people of Israel that the alien and the Jew were equal in God's eyes. All people were created by God and all were to be treated equally (Numbers 15:15). Christians should oppose racism and discrimination and live in such a way that people of all races will be drawn to God's redemptive, nonracist love.

Outside Activity:

Ask the students to keep a list of observations about race relations at their schools and in their communities for one week. This can be an inventory of both positive and negative accounts of race relations. When the group gathers again, people can share their observations and make personal commitments to fight racism.

GOD THOUGHTS

1 How often do you think about God? (Circle one.)

a. All of the time   **c.** Hardly ever

b. Sometimes   **d.** God who?

2 Underline the word pictures that you feel best describe how God seems to you. You may choose three.

The big policeman in the sky   **The guilt guy**

A wimp   **The supreme being**

A nice old man   **A rock and roll party dude**

A sleep-over kind of friend   **The lifeguard upstairs**

A spectacular super hero   **A sinless big saint**

The cosmic Santa Claus   **The God of my folks**

3 Answer the following question: **How is God like a parent?**

_____

_____

Place an X on the line below, indicating which direction you are moving in your relationship with God.

|_____|_____|_____| |_____|_____|_____|_____|_____|

Closer to God   **Away from God**

4 How do you feel your relationship with God is affected by your God thoughts (your concept of God)?

_____

_____

5 **Romans 11:33-36** describes God, and **Romans 12:1, 2** tells us what we should do because of who God is. Summarize each of the passages below.

Romans 11:33-36 _____

_____

_____

Romans 12:1, 2 _____

_____

_____

GOD THOUGHTS
Topic: Views of God

Purpose of this Session:

John 1:18 says that "no one has ever seen God," yet the Bible is filled with metaphorical descriptions of him. This TalkSheet helps your kids explore their conceptions of God through discussion.

To Introduce the Topic:

Although some preparation is required, this can be a fun introductory strategy. You will need five balloons and five slips of paper. Write one of the following questions on each of the papers:

1. If God were to visit your church, where would he sit?
2. What color of hair do you think God has?
3. If God were to talk with you audibly, what tone of voice would he use?
4. What is the funniest looking animal God might say he created?
5. What do you think God does for fun?

   Place one of these slips in each balloon, then blow up and tie the balloons. At the beginning of your meeting, choose five young people to participate in this activity. Bring them to the front of the group and give each a balloon. Tell them to sit on the balloons to pop them. They must then respond to the statements on their slips of paper.

The Discussion:

Item #1: Get an overall average of how often your kids think of God. Ask how their view of God has changed since they were children.

Item #2: Let kids share their pictures of God. If they think of additional pictures, encourage them to share these as well.

Item #3: Answers will vary depending upon their parents' style of parenting. Make a list of all the ways God is like a parent. Turn the table and list all the ways God is not like a parent. This will give your group a more accurate concept of God.

Item #4: Our God thoughts have a profound influence on our relationship with him. If you view God as mean, it may be difficult to have a close personal friendship. If you see God as forgiving and warm, then you may share more with him. Probe with the kids how they feel their relationship with God is affected by their God thoughts.

Item #5: Emphasize the connection between who God is (Romans 11:33-36) and what our natural response will be (Romans 12:1, 2) if we fully understand God.

To Close the Session:

Challenge the group to rethink its view of God. Most of us have a small perception of God. Our God thoughts limit what God can do in our lives. God commanded us not to worship idols (Exodus 20:3-6) because he knew that our distorted views of him would limit what he could do with us and what we could do with him. Suggest to the students that every time they find something about God in the Bible that they write a large "G" in the margin. Then every time they open their Bibles they will begin to see descriptions of God that they can review.

Outside Activities:

1. Ask the kids to pick five Bible stories. Then have them study the stories and write down five new things they learned about God.

2. Have the group members make a list of adjectives they think best describe God, along with scriptural support for their lists. The students can compare their lists and together develop a picture of God.

ALCOHOL AND OTHER DRUGS

Young people my age say no to alcohol and other drugs.

___ **TRUE for most young people at my school.**
___ **NOT TRUE for most young people at my school.**

A "gateway drug" is a drug that gets people started doing more and more drugs. Look at the following list of drugs. Circle the three that you believe are the three most used gateway or starter drugs for young people in your community.

Alcohol	**Tobacco**
LSD	**Heroin**
Caffeine	**Marijuana**
Speed	**Inhalants**
Cocaine	**Downers**

Why are the gateway or starter drugs you identified in Item #2 sometimes used by young people your age? (Check the top three reasons.)

___ They are easy to get.   ___ You feel like an adult.
___ They don't seem harmful.   ___ They are inexpensive to get.
___ It's fun.   ___ It's part of growing up.
___ It's exciting.   ___ It's expected.
___ It's cool if you do them.   ___ Everyone else is doing them.

Check (✓) the five best reasons for you as a young person to avoid alcohol and other drugs.

___ I don't want to disappoint my parents.   ___ I want to prevent harm to my body.
___ I want to stay close to God.   ___ I don't want to get into trouble.
___ I don't want to get addicted.   ___ I don't want to go against what I believe.
___ I wouldn't want to lose my friends.   ___ I don't want to have problems in the future.
___ I don't want to get arrested.   ___ I want to live up to my full potential.

Circle the statement or statements below that describe the best ways to avoid alcohol and other drug use.

a. Choose friends who don't use.   **g.** Avoid places where people drink/use drugs.
b. Just say no.   **h.** Tell people you don't drink.
c. Pray regularly.   **i.** If you do use, only use a little bit.
d. Don't go to parties.   **j.** Talk with your parents about suggestions.
e. Practice saying no.   **k.** Tell people you are a Christian.
f. Take healthy risks to have fun in life.

Decide which of the following passages is the most helpful in dealing personally with the issue of alcohol and drugs. Circle the Scripture you chose.

Proverbs 3:7, 8	**Proverbs 23:19-21**	**Luke 8:11-15**
1 Corinthians 3:16, 17	**2 Corinthians 13:5, 6**	**Romans 14:21**
Galatians 6:7, 8		

ALCOHOL AND OTHER DRUGS
Topic: Drug Use

Purpose of this Session:

Young people are experimenting with substances at younger ages. When looking at junior highers/middle schoolers, it is easy to be fooled because they do not look like a group that would want to try drugs. But many of them are. And those that aren't are feeling the pressure to do so. This TalkSheet purposely includes alcohol and drugs so that young people will understand that there is not a difference. This is not to suggest that adults shouldn't drink in moderation. But adults as well as young people need to understand that when they drink they are consuming a legal drug. Take the opportunity to talk with your young people about drugs and how they can avoid them.

To Introduce the Topic:

Tell your group you are all going to make up a story about drinking and drugging. Ask the group members to keep their contributions clean. Begin by saying, "It was after school and mom was at work. So . . ." then have a young person add the next part of the plot. Let volunteers keep the story going. You are sure to end up with an introduction to the topic of drug and alcohol use.

   Another good lead-in is to ask the kids to name all the sports figures they know who have had problems with drinking and/or drugs. If you have many group members who are sports enthusiasts, you will be able to create a long list of names. Ask the group why these sports heroes became involved in drinking and drugging.

The Discussion:

Item #1: The answers your young people give will provide you with your group's perspective on the pressure to use and how many kids are using. Many kids will say it is a problem for others but not for them. You have the chance through this discussion to explore ways to keep it from becoming a problem in the future.

Item #2: Explain how drugs like caffeine, tobacco, and alcohol orient kids toward chemicals. We have created a culture that finds pleasure through chemicals and avoids pain by medicating through alcohol and drugs. And gateway chemicals are the introduction.

Item #3: Create a master list of reasons young people use gateway drugs. Ask them to identify all of the good reasons from the master list. Point out how false and deceptive these reasons are.

Item #4: Here the group can focus upon good reasons to avoid use. Reach a group consensus for the best reasons to stay clean.

Item #5: Take time to role-play tough situations that the kids identify as possibilities they may face. Kids need to practice refusal skills so that they will be prepared to handle difficult situations.

Item #6: Ask volunteers to identify the most helpful passage. If some young people did not find any of the verses helpful, ask them to search the Scriptures for stories and passages they find helpful.

To Close the Session:

Emphasize that you understand how difficult are the temptations your young people face in relation to all of the drugs available. Affirm the students that in Christ they have the power to overcome these temptations (1 Corinthians 10:13; James 1:12-15). Ask several volunteers to review what was discussed, then offer the group your personal convictions. Invite several of the parents to attend the group to share their convictions as well, using biblical references.

Outside Activity:

Ask an adult Christian and a teenager recovering from chemical dependency to discuss addiction and recovery. Advise the guest speakers that you do not want the alcohol and drug usage to be glamorized and glorified. Often speakers tell funny stories of when they were using, then only briefly talk about their addictions and struggles with recovery.

WALKIN' WITH GOD

1 Your relationship with God is the most important relationship you have.

___ **True for me** ___ **Sometimes true for me** ___ **Not true for me**

2 Write something about how you might feel if you were told . . .

a. you could not have a close relationship with God.

_____

b. you could never again attend church.

_____

c. you were wasting your time on this Christian stuff.

_____

3 When do you feel closest to God? (Circle your answers.)

During the church worship service	When I think about heaven
At camps and retreats	During Communion, the Lord's Supper
When I pray by myself	While reading the Bible
During Sunday school	On holidays
When I am in trouble	Almost anytime I am at church
No particular time	Never

4 Draw a cross next to the following things you believe would help you develop a friendship with God.

___ Regularly attend church	___ Take Communion
___ Watch TV evangelists	___ Accept God's acceptance of you just the way you are
___ Talk with God every day	___ Keep all of God's rules
___ Try really hard to please God	___ Spend time with other Christians
___ Spend time alone with God	___ Reach out to help others in the name of Christ
___ Thank God regularly for all the things he does for you	___ Worry that God will punish you for your sins
___ Feel guilty a lot	___ Learn more about God by reading the Bible
	___ Listen to God

5 Read each of the following verses that describe something about Jesus Christ's humanness. After each passage write out what you learned about the humanity of the Lord.

Matthew 26:37 _____

Luke 2:40 _____

Luke 4:2 _____

Luke 8:23 _____

Luke 24:39 _____

John 4:6 _____

Date Used: _____   Group: _____

WALKIN' WITH GOD
Topic: Knowing God More Personally

Purpose of this Session:

We all desire personal relationships. During the young teen years, close friendships are vitally important. Also during the teen years, the adolescent's conception of God changes. With the ability for reflective thought comes the ability to think of God in more personal terms. Take this chance to talk with your group about knowing God more personally.

To Introduce the Topic:

For this activity you will need markers and a large sheet of paper. The paper should be taped to a wall where the group can see it. With suggestions from the group, ask one young person to draw a picture of God. Try to incorporate all of the suggestions into your drawing. Kids will say things like "white hair," "beard," "wrinkles," "wise eyes," and "really tall." Stop after a few minutes of drawing to discuss if this is a picture of the God with whom they have or would like to have a relationship. Then pass out the TalkSheets and announce that you will be talking about how to know God more personally.

The Discussion:

Item #1: You will not find the phrase "personal relationship with Jesus Christ" in the Bible. Yet we can talk about a personal relationship with Christ because he so often used personal metaphors of friend, family member, and marriage. Ask the kids what they think it means to have a personal relationship with God.

Item #2: This activity lets kids examine how significant their relationship with God really is. Each of these negative mandates strikes at their personal relationship with God.

Item #3: Let kids add additional times they feel close to God that are not on the list. Ask the group why these times are special times with God.

Item #4: Ask each kid to create a plan for knowing God more personally based upon what is learned as people share their lists. Explore ways the group can together develop a more personal relationship with God.

Item #5: God became man because he wanted to have a relationship with us. Too often we dwell on God's divinity rather than his humanity. By focusing for a minute on God's humanness, young people can appreciate the personal side of God. Read and discuss Hebrews 4:15, 16.

To Close the Session:

Point out to the group that the metaphor of "walking with God" is a useful way to look at how we relate to him. There are different ways we walk with people. For example, if you go to the mall with your parents, you might walk away from them. You don't want your friends to see you so close to them. When walking with a boyfriend or a girlfriend, you might hold hands or walk arm in arm. If you have the unfortunate experience of walking with a police officer to be questioned for a crime, you might walk with your head lowered. While with your friends, you might walk casually and coolly as you talk. Ask the kids to describe how they are walking with God. Then read the following bumper sticker to them: "If you don't feel close to God, guess who moved."

Outside Activity:

Encourage your group members to keep spiritual journals of their relationships with God. For one week they are to write down their thoughts and feelings about God. Times good for journaling would be as they pray, read the Bible, worship, or reflect in the evening on the day with God. They may want to write a poem, compose a prayer, draw a picture, or write a narrative. At your next meeting, kids can share their thoughts and feelings about their journaling experiences. Some of them may find they enjoy journaling and will continue to do so.

GROUND ZERO

1 Do you believe a nuclear war could destroy civilization?

___ Yes

___ No

___ Maybe

___ Don't know

2 Have you ever . . .

	YES	NO	MAYBE
a. worried about a nuclear war happening in your lifetime?	___	___	___
b. thought about what it would be like if you survived a nuclear war?	___	___	___
c. wondered what God thinks about nuclear weapons?	___	___	___

3 How often have you talked with your parents about the possibility of a nuclear war? (Circle one answer.)

Never   **At least once**   **More than once**

4 Do you believe the world is a safer place in which to live because of nuclear weapons?

____ Yes   ____ No   ____ Maybe

5 Do you **AGREE** or **DISAGREE** with the statements below?

	AGREE	DISAGREE
a. People need to learn more about the threat of nuclear war.	___	___
b. The Bible has nothing to say about nuclear war.	___	___
c. The threat of nuclear war is one of the biggest problems faced by today's world.	___	___
d. There is nothing that can be done to prevent nuclear war.	___	___
e. Nuclear weapons could be used on a limited scale without getting out of hand.	___	___
f. The church should speak out against the threat of nuclear war.	___	___

6 Read the following verses and summarize each in five words or less.

Psalm 34:14 _____

Proverbs 12:20 _____

Matthew 5:9 _____

Romans 12:18 _____

GROUND ZERO
Topic: Nuclear War

Purpose of this Session:

The world possesses the ability to destroy itself. Young people growing up under the shadow of nuclear proliferation express anxiety and fears regarding the threat of this nuclear destruction, depending upon what crisis is occurring. Talking about this issue as well as our Christian hope in Christ and our peacemaking mandate can help young people deal positively with their anxieties.

To Introduce the Topic:

Break the group into four smaller groups placed strategically around the room. Tell each group it represents a country. Be sure to appoint one country to be a Christian nation. Place a table at each group and a table in the middle of the room to represent the United Nations. Any country can send a representative to any other country by going to another's table. When any one country wants to talk to all the countries, it can call a meeting of the United Nations and all countries must gather at the middle table. Give each group an envelope that contains information about its country. Keep the information brief, but mention the number of nuclear weapons it has, the wealth it possesses, and the level of democracy that exists. Tape a list of each country's information on the United Nations table for all the countries to see. Give each country a minute to talk briefly about its information and to select a president, an ambassador to each other country, and a United Nations representative.

Announce that one of the countries has been attacked by another, using nuclear weapons. Tell both the attacking country and the attacked country who they are. Give the attacking country an 8 1/2 x 11 piece of paper and ask the group to write down the extent of damage done to the attacked country. As moderator, you are allowed to mediate this process and deny any damages. Keep the damages to a minimum at the beginning of the game to allow this simulation to last a while. Tape the damage list with the name of the attacking country to the attacked country's table. Keep the game going by allowing the attacked country as well as the other countries to decide what they will do. Facilitate this process until you are satisfied that the young people have learned something about nuclear war.

You can discuss the activity by asking what difference Christian principles made, what difference nuclear weapons made, and what happened during the course of the game.

The Discussion:

Item #1: Let the young people share their opinions. You can refer to what happened during the simulation game used to introduce this topic.

Item #2: Kids will have stories that they have considered and watched in the movies. Focus on what the young people believe God thinks about nuclear weapons.

Item #3: The nuclear threat is one of the least talked about topics between parent and child. Many of the young people will not know what their parents believe. Ask them if they would be willing to take this TalkSheet home and discuss it with their parents.

Item #4: Ask the kids what they think would make the world a safer place in which to live.

Item #5: Take a poll on each of these statements. Let the young people debate the more controversial issues.

Item #6: After studying the Scriptures, have the young people choose one to memorize. They can then repeat the Scripture to themselves when they next find themselves in a situation where peace is needed.

To Close the Session:

Explain that fears and concerns about nuclear proliferation and war are normal. As Christians we can be confident knowing that God is in control of the nations. If we survey the Old Testament, we can clearly see that God was in control of history even though it did not always appear that way to his people. Today God wants us to work for peace. This can begin in your own backyard. You can be a peacemaker at home, at school, in your neighborhood, on your sports team, and at church.

Outside Activities:

1. Ask several adults of different ages to attend the group and talk about how they have coped with their fears of nuclear weapons.

2. Ask the young people to make a list of all the violent movies they watch, including war movies. Then ask them if these may be contributing to the increase in violence in our culture. Challenge them to not expose themselves to this sort of violence if they wish to be peacemakers for Christ.

GETTING GOOD AT CHURCH

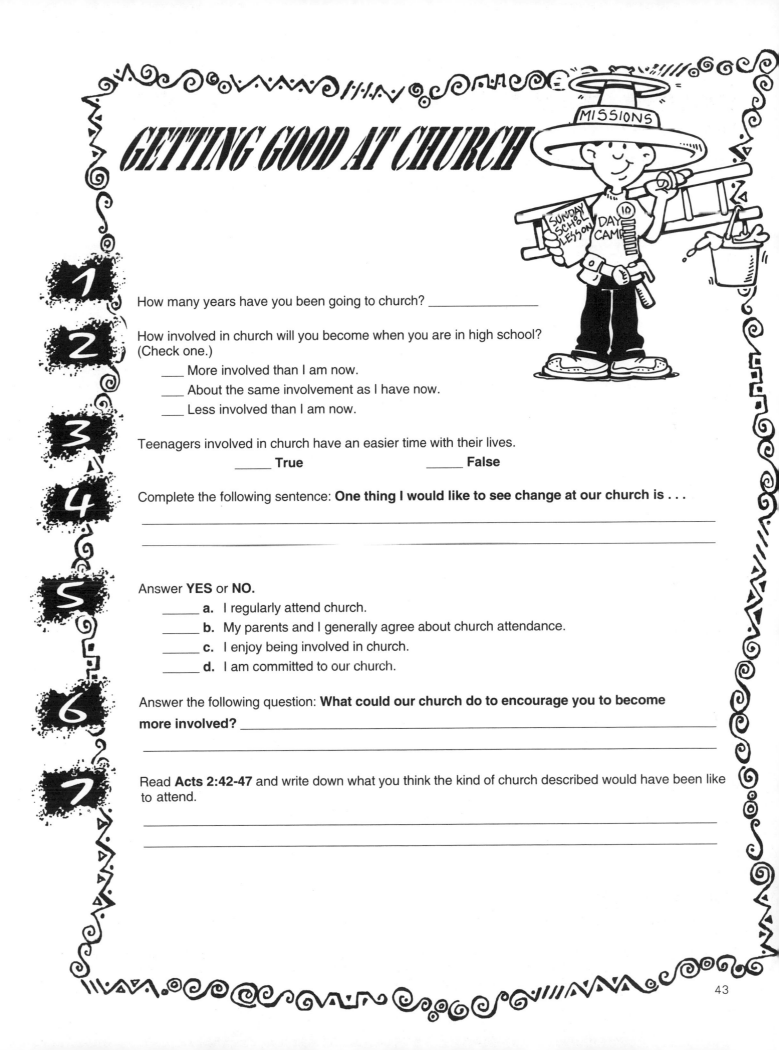

1 How many years have you been going to church? _____

2 How involved in church will you become when you are in high school? (Check one.)

___ More involved than I am now.

___ About the same involvement as I have now.

___ Less involved than I am now.

3 Teenagers involved in church have an easier time with their lives.

_____ **True**   _____ **False**

4 Complete the following sentence: **One thing I would like to see change at our church is . . .**

_____

_____

5 Answer **YES** or **NO**.

_____ **a.** I regularly attend church.

_____ **b.** My parents and I generally agree about church attendance.

_____ **c.** I enjoy being involved in church.

_____ **d.** I am committed to our church.

6 Answer the following question: **What could our church do to encourage you to become more involved?** _____

_____

7 Read **Acts 2:42-47** and write down what you think the kind of church described would have been like to attend.

_____

_____

GETTING GOOD AT CHURCH
Topic: Church Involvement

Purpose of this Session:

Church is something that has not been a choice for many of your young people. Since day one they have been attending. But now they are fast approaching an age where they can make a choice about their involvement. Some of your kids love church involvement. Others do everything they can to get out of it. If they are like most, your kids are at different stages of church commitment. Use this TalkSheet to talk about church involvement in a nonthreatening manner. Let kids who are openly rebelling against attending church speak their minds. Let young people who are excited and actively involved share their stories and encourage the discouraged and angry. Maintain an open environment where the Holy Spirit can work in the lives of everyone no matter what their commitment.

To Introduce the Topic:

Here is an introductory activity that will encourage some creative thought from your kids about how they see the church. Divide into groups of four or five. Give each group an item like a coat hanger, a chair, an eraser, or a roll of masking tape. Ask each group to think up a one-statement slogan that describes the church. For example, if the item were a coat hanger, the group might say something like "Church is like a coat hanger; if you use it, you have less wrinkles in your life." If you choose not to hand out specific items, you can ask the group to come up with a slogan using any item. For example, a group may say "Church is like a mobile phone; whenever you need it, it's there." You can then hand out the TalkSheets and announce the topic.

Another fun introduction is to divide your kids into small groups and have a contest to see which group can come up with the best excuses for missing church. Give the groups three minutes to work. Ask them to share some of the most "interesting" ones.

The Discussion:

Item #1: Total up everyone's years for a grand total of years. It might be fun for the kids to estimate how many sermons they have sat through. Then ask how many they remember.

Item #2: Ask young people to provide reasons for their responses. Identify the trend in your group. Are most expecting to exit or get more involved?

Item #3: Here is a practical Christianity statement. Make a list of all the ways church kids have an easier time as well as a list of ways church kids have a tougher time.

Item #4: Do not let this turn into a gripe session, but make it an opportunity for young people to give their input and suggest creative ways they could be God's change agents.

Item #5: Take a poll on each of these four statements. Then talk about what your group thinks makes a church good.

Item #6: After group members share their responses, turn the question around and ask what the young people can do for the church to encourage more teenager involvement.

Item #7: Ask young people to share their answers about involvement in the first-century church. Then ask the group what Christians from the first-century church might say if they were to have a chance to be involved in today's church.

To Close the Session:

Close this session with a brainstorming activity. Ask the kids to create a list of all the benefits of being involved in church as a teenager. Focus on worship, service opportunities, fun times, and personal Christian growth activities. This simple activity can help your young people identify all of the positive opportunities available that they had not ever considered.

Outside Activity:

Windshield flyers have long been used as a way to advertise an event, a product, or a program. You can also use the production of a flyer as an additional discussion activity. You will need sheets of construction paper, markers, and some sample business flyers. Explain to your group that it is in charge of publicity for a church. The kids can first create a church situation. Let them be as imaginative as they wish as long as it is a church that could realistically exist. Then they should design a windshield flyer that advertises the church of their creation. You can then have each group share its flyer and talk a little bit about its dream church.

THE D WORD

1 How often have you thought about death?

___ **Many times**   ___ **A few times**   ___ **Never**

2 The following prayer has been popular with children for many years. Why do you think this prayer about death is prayed by kids with their parents?

_____

_____

Now I lay me down to sleep,

I pray the Lord my soul to keep.

And if I die before I wake,

I pray the Lord my soul to take.

3 Brian died of leukemia last Thursday night. He attended your church and was very active in youth group. His seventh grade homeroom class found out ten minutes ago. Even though they knew he would die because of the disease, the class was still in disbelief about his death.

What is one thing you would tell the class to help them cope with Brian's death?

_____

_____

_____

4 Death is a natural part of the life cycle.

_____ **True**   _____ **False**

5 What is one question you always wanted to ask about death?

_____

_____

_____

6 Carefully read **1 Corinthians 15:54-58** to see what it teaches Christians about death.

THE D WORD
Topic: Death

Purpose of this Session:

Death is a topic that more and more must be talked about with kids. An increasing number of young people are preoccupied with death—in their music, through the suicide of a classmate, and in the contemplation of the meaning and purpose of life. In their desire to protect young people or in their own denial of death, many adults avoid the subject, especially with children and young adolescents. This TalkSheet faces death in a straightforward manner. By talking about the thought of death, you are provided with the opportunity to talk about eternal salvation.

To Introduce the Topic:

Play the game "Killer" to get the group talking about the subject of death. Have everyone sit in a circle in chairs or on the floor and face inward. Ask the kids to close their eyes and bow their heads. Walk around the inner circle and tap one player on the head. That player is now "the killer." Sit down and ask the young people to raise their heads and open their eyes. Play begins by everyone looking around at each other and talking casually. The killer "kills" people by winking at them. When a person is winked at (killed), that player waits five seconds and falls over dead. Once someone is winked at, he or she is dead and cannot reveal to the group who winked. Anyone who suspects the killer is allowed to guess, but anyone making a wrong guess is also dead. If someone is asked if he or she is the killer, that person must answer truthfully. The killer tries to see how many people she or he can pick off before getting caught. Whoever catches the killer gets to pick the next killer.

The Discussion:

Item #1: Many kids will share the experiences they have had with death, such as the death of a grandparent or a pet. Or perhaps they will talk about the suicide of a classmate or the death and destruction themes of rock music. Be sensitive to young people who are mourning the loss of friends and family after a death. Allow kids to share their stories and express their emotions.

Item #2: Take this opportunity to talk about the apparent meaninglessness of death. Explain to the group that the Bible has a lot to say about death. Death was brought into the world because of sin (Romans 5:12; Romans 6:23). The prayer was written at a time when death was more real to young people because the medical treatments available today had not yet been invented and many young people died in childhood. They could not understand the tragedy of death any more than we can, but they knew it was a result of sin and they knew they needed salvation.

Item #3: Ask them to share the responses they would give the students to help them cope with Brian's death. Ask if sharing the life-changing message of Jesus Christ is something that would help.

Item #4: The New Testament (Romans 5:12-14; 1 Corinthians 15:26) teaches that death is our enemy, although we need not fear it. It is not a part of the natural life cycle. Death proves the reality of sin and evil.

Item #5: Answer as many questions as you have time for. Remind the group that there is no such thing as a stupid question. Expect a wide variety of questions from mortuaries and cremation to what happens to people right after they die, reincarnation, and more.

Item #6: Study the passage together. Focus upon the Christian's hope in death (our Saviour, Jesus Christ) and our response to this hope (stand firm and serve the Lord).

To Close the Session:

Review the ground the group has covered. Use this closing time to point out that the life of each individual involved in this TalkSheet discussion has meaning. It is God who gives our lives meaning. Because of Christ's work on the Cross of Calvary, each of us can be saved from the despair of a meaningless life and ultimate death. Death stares all of us in the face. We may try to turn our backs on it through the pursuit of pleasure or hard work, but death cannot be denied forever. Through the salvation offered by the Lord Jesus Christ, we can pass from death to life—a life everlasting (John 5:24).

The media sensationalize death to the point that nearly all deaths are violent, unbelievable, or dramatic. As a result, young people are desensitized regarding death. It is almost viewed as an unreal occurrence, only happening to an unfortunate few. But death is very real. The new age movement has anesthetized people to the reality of death with its focus on reincarnation and testimonials of near death experiences of people not fearing death. They report moving toward a light, coaxed on by a mysterious guide, and of seeing loved ones who have died. This denial of the finality and tragedy of death brought on by sin only serves to confuse young people. Only through a relationship with Jesus Christ can death be viewed realistically.

Outside Activity:

Ask a funeral home director to talk with your group about her or his experiences with families who have had a loved one die. The students can also ask questions about everything from embalming to burial.

FRIENDSHIP FACTS

1 Answer these questions.

a. What do you like the most about your friends?

_____

_____

b. What do you like the least about your friends?

_____

_____

2 Your parents should have a say in your choice of friends. (Check one.)

___ **I could live with that** ___ **Maybe sometimes** ___ **Never**

3 **TRUE** or **FALSE** for me: The friends I have try to influence me to do things I know are wrong.

_____ **True** _____ **False**

4 For each of the following situations, give your advice.

SITUATION	ADVICE

a. "I have a friend who lies to me about big
as well as little things. I'm not sure I want
to lose her friendship because she is popular."

b. "My group of friends makes fun of me. I think
they do it just for laughs. I have told them I don't
like it, but that has not made them stop."

c. "I just moved here from out of state. I find it
difficult to make friends. My mom says to make
friends I have to be a friend. Give me a break—I
need some advice that really works."

d. "I have a friend who is doing something wrong. I don't
want to say what it is, but I do want to help my friend."

e. "There are three different groups of friends at my church.
I quit going because I can't break into any of the groups."

5 Decide which of the following passages describe friendship and which do not.

1 Samuel 18:1	Job 19:19	Mark 14:50	John 5:7	John 15:13
Romans 1:11, 12	Philippians 2:25	1 Timothy 1:16, 17	2 Timothy 4:10	

FRIENDSHIP FACTS
Topic: Friends

Purpose of this Session:

Family can only go so far in providing for the needs of kids. Young teens crave friendship. Since friends can teach young people so much, the friendships they establish can literally make or break their adolescent years. Use this TalkSheet as an opportunity to talk about this vitally critical area. You can create a positive discussion with the young people in your group about a topic that most kids refuse to talk about with their parents.

To Introduce the Topic:

For this activity you will need construction paper, pens, glue, magazines, markers, yarn, and other decorations. Pass out a sheet of construction paper to each person in the group. Tell them they are to make a friendship card. The front of it may be decorated in any fashion along the lines of friendship. On the inside of the card, they can write a poem, a letter, a story, words, or artwork about friends or friendship. Collect the cards when they are finished and choose a "delivery person" to pass out the cards. Make sure no one gets the card he or she made. Allow the group members time to read their cards. The cards may be kept by the people receiving them or exchanged with others. Then pass out copies of the TalkSheets and announce the discussion topic will be friendship.

Another approach to introducing this topic is to tell the young people they will be creating a "recipe of friendship." Hand out a copy of a conventional recipe (like chocolate chip cookies). You can also write this on a chalkboard or a large sheet of paper. Break into small groups and explain that they are each to invent a recipe for friendship using this format. It might be helpful to brainstorm and write down all the words the group can think of that would apply to friendship. Words such as *love, caring, honesty, trustworthy, confront, share,* and so on may be suggested for the groups to choose from as they write their recipes. Encourage their uniqueness and creativity. When the recipes are completed, have the group members exchange recipes and each one read a recipe to the group.

The Discussion:

Item #1: Create a master list of likes and dislikes. Circle those qualities that are mentioned more than once. Ask the group what they plan to do with the qualities they like the least. Are these characteristics we all share? Are they things that can be overlooked? Should they be overlooked?

Item #2: Young people are usually very defensive when friends and parents are mentioned in the same sentence. Most will say parents should have no say. Brainstorm ways the young people can choose their own friends and still maintain dialogue with their parents.

Item #3: Ask the young people to provide reasons for their responses. Ask how often they influence their friends to do the wrong things.

Item #4: You can pass out 3 x 5 cards and let kids write their own situations and answer them as a group.

Item #5: Ask the kids to share their answers. Have them identify some of the characteristics of friendship and friendlessness found in the passages.

To Close the Session:

Summarize the points that have been made during the TalkSheet discussion. Point out to the group that to have friends you must be a friend. Ask volunteers to role-play some different types of people and let the group decide if these would make good friends. The group can identify the types of individuals that can be role-played. Close by talking about how God wants to be our friend. Everyone can have a personal relationship with Christ.

Outside Activity:

Obtain the names and addresses of the kids in another youth group. This group may be either across town or across the country. Have each member of your group choose a name of the same sex and write a letter of introduction to his or her new pen pal.

THE HEAVENS AND THE EARTH

1 Have you ever wondered if God really did create the heavens and the earth?

____ **Many times**
____ **A couple of times**
____ **One time**
____ **Never**

2 Science will prove the Bible to be wrong! (Check only one response.)

____ **Eventually**   ____ **I doubt it**   ____ **No way**

3 A person cannot be a Christian and believe in evolution.

____ **True**   ____ **False**

4 What should Christians do when they are taught something in school that they think might be contrary to what the Bible teaches? (You may circle more than one.)

a. Carefully examine the facts.
b. Believe everything you are taught.
c. Ask someone you trust for his or her opinion.
d. Compare what the Bible says with what you are being taught.
e. Be close minded.
f. Search for the truth.
g. Pray for God's guidance.

5 Try to answer the following two questions.

a. What is the most difficult thing to accept about the theory of evolution?

_____

_____

b. What is the most difficult thing to accept about what the Bible says about creation?

_____

_____

6 Read each of the following passages of Scripture and write a one word feeling about each of them.

Exodus 20:8-11 _____

Psalm 19:1-6 _____

Revelation 14:7 _____

THE HEAVENS AND THE EARTH
Topic: Science and Creation

Purpose of this Session:

Christian young people progressing through school are confronted with questions and doubts about the validity of their religious upbringing because it appears to conflict with what they learn in their science classes. This TalkSheet encourages an open and honest discussion on the subjects of science and creation. Be sure you set the tone for Christian love, open-mindedness, and safety as young people share their doubts and concerns.

To Introduce the Topic:

Bring in a toy and a large rock and set them both before the group. Ask the group to describe how both came into existence. After discussing this, point out that it is easy for us to see that someone had to create the toy. Yet many people have difficulty believing that a Creator had to make the rock. Then tell the group you will be discussing the issues of science and creation.

The Discussion:

Item #1: Ask the young people to share some of the wonders and questions they have had about creation.

Item #2: Point out to the group that technically science can never really prove the Bible wrong because there is no scientific statement that can ever be considered absolutely true. In science, what is thought to be correct thinking one day gets thrown out the window the next when new data are analyzed.

Item #3: This unfortunately has been a litmus test for some Christians. The Bible is clear, however, regarding admission into God's kingdom (Acts 16:31).

Item #4: Ask the young people to share realistically what they would do. Then brainstorm with the group additional ideas for handling difficult situations.

Item #5: Give young people the chance to share their doubts and still retain their faith. When we discount doubting, we often push kids further away from faith in God rather than encouraging their faith.

Item #6: Read each of the passages and after each ask volunteers to share the words they wrote. Make a list of the words that describe God's miracle of creation.

To Close the Session:

It is beyond the scope of this TalkSheet to discuss the details of the theories of evolution and creation. If you are well versed in these theories, you can debate the merits of each. The point that needs to be made is that God has declared his involvement in creation—in its beginning, sustenance, and end. The atheistic interpretations of God's creation or the new age pantheistic interpretations inadequately answer the order, wonder, and complexity of God's creation. Only a view that includes the God of the Bible can adequately explain our world and everything in it. Explain that one has to have as much faith in science to believe its theories as one does to believe in the Bible. Close by reading Psalm 100.

Outside Activity:

Ask a scientist or science teacher who is a Christian to present the different perspectives on the creation/evolution debate.

BUT I DON'T FEEL CALLED

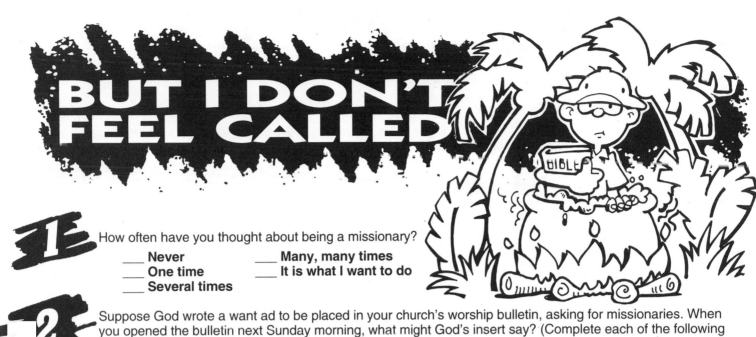

 **1** How often have you thought about being a missionary?

___ Never   ___ Many, many times
___ One time   ___ It is what I want to do
___ Several times

2 Suppose God wrote a want ad to be placed in your church's worship bulletin, asking for missionaries. When you opened the bulletin next Sunday morning, what might God's insert say? (Complete each of the following sentences.)

WANTED! CHRISTIAN MISSIONARIES

You will need to know _____.

You must want to _____.

It would be nice if _____.

You must be able to _____.

3 Underline three of the following things you would like our group to do.

Regularly pray for a specific missionary.
Write letters to a missionary.
Have a Bible study about missions and missionaries.
Go on a missions trip.
Work on a missions project each month.
Watch a video about missions.
Send money or materlals to a missionary.
Find out what our church's missions program is doing.

4 Do you **AGREE** or **DISAGREE** with the following statements?

	AGREE	DISAGREE
a. One must be a super-spiritual saint to be a missionary.	___	___
b. God's favorite work is missionary work.	___	___
c. Only nerds become missionaries.	___	___
d. It is a privilege to serve Christ as a missionary.	___	___
e. Most people in today's world are already Christians.	___	___
f. Our church already does enough missions stuff.	___	___

 5 Why would God want you to be a missionary? _____

_____

_____

6 Read **Acts 1:8**. This is the cause you are now living for. How will you do it? _____

_____

_____

Date Used: _____   Group: _____

BUT I DON'T FEEL CALLED
Topic: Missions and Missionaries

Purpose of this Session:

Young people often like to hear exciting adventure stories about missionaries, but they do not picture themselves living them out. You can expand your group's missions worldview by using this TalkSheet to discuss key issues in the missionary endeavor. Christian young people can and need to understand their part in taking the life-changing message of Jesus Christ to all the world.

To Introduce the Topic:

Tell your kids they are all going to make up a progressive story about missionaries. Begin the story by saying, "In a far off country there was a group of missionaries who . . ." then let a young person proceed with the plot, continuing around the group. The only rules are that the story should be kept clean and that it be about missionaries. Many of the myths that persist about missionaries will make their way into the story. You will end up with a crazy story and a good lead-in to the discussion.

The Discussion:

Item #1: After getting several kids in the group to share their responses, ask them to consider what it might be like to be a missionary. What would a common day look like? How do missionaries have fun? Do missionaries ever sin? All these and more might be questions you ask your group.

Item #2: This item further considers what it is like to be a missionary. Create a master list that can be sent to missionaries supported by your church for their appraisal.

Item #3: Here you have introduced the group to various missions-oriented opportunities. Explore the commitment level of each of the tasks. You may want to wait until you wrap up the discussion before calling the group to commit to any specific tasks.

Item #4: Consider each of the statements and how they apply to winning the world for Christ.

Item #5: Tell the group that all Christians are missionaries—some are just better at it than others. Ask the group to explore what it might be like to trust God and choose missionary work as a career goal.

Item #6: Collect a number of ideas as to how Acts 1:8 can be lived out in junior high/middle school.

To Close the Session:

Challenge the students to consider how they can be involved in missionary work. Explain to them the Great Commission found in Matthew 28:18-20. Introduce them to the concept of the "World Christian." David Bryant defines World Christians as "day-to-day disciples for whom Christ's global cause has become the integrating, overriding priority for all that He is for them." * World Christians take the Great Commission given by Christ seriously. The kids can be World Christians if they make the Great Commission a very important part of their lives.

Outside Activity:

Invite the young people to write down questions they have about missions and missionaries. Then send these to several of the missionaries your church supports. Read the missionaries' responses when you receive them.

   Ridge Burns has put together an exciting book to help your group get into the missions field: *The Complete Student Missions Handbook* (Youth Specialties/Zondervan, 1990). Review his book to see how your group can get involved.

* David Bryant, *In the Gap: What It Means to Be a World Christian* (Downers Grove, Ill.: InterVarsity Christian Fellowship, 1979), 63.

PEER POWER

1 The average teenager will rebel against his or her parents.

_____ **Yes** _____ **No**

2 If you had a really important decision to make or a problem to resolve in your life, would you most likely go to your parents or to your friends for advice?

_____ **My parents** _____ **My friends**

Why? _____

_____

3 Who would you most likely go to for each of the following?

a. If you had a problem with a friend.   _____ **PARENT** _____ **FRIEND**

b. If you felt bad about something you had done wrong. _____ **PARENT** _____ **FRIEND**

c. If you had a question about sex.   _____ **PARENT** _____ **FRIEND**

d. If you wondered what clothes to buy.   _____ **PARENT** _____ **FRIEND**

e. If you had a problem at school.   _____ **PARENT** _____ **FRIEND**

f. If you were offered a drink of alcohol.   _____ **PARENT** _____ **FRIEND**

g. If you wondered what sport to play.   _____ **PARENT** _____ **FRIEND**

4 Young people's friends have more influence on them than their parents do.

_____ This has usually been **true** for me.

_____ This has usually **not been true** for me.

5 Read each of the following Bible verses and decide if it is an example of a good influence or a not so good influence. Place the verses under the correct heading.

GOOD STUFF **NOT SO GOOD STUFF**

Genesis 13:12, 13

Genesis 13:18

2 Kings 17:28

2 Kings 17:34

Psalm 1:1, 2

Psalm 1:4, 5

Proverbs 1:7-9

Proverbs 1:10-16

PEER POWER
Topic: The Influence of Parents and Peers

Purpose of this Session:

Parents are the number one influence on young people. Yet the peer group gains increasing importance in the lives of young adolescents. This is one of the biggest fears parents have, since they see how influential the peer group can be. One of your responsibilities as a youth leader is to affirm the role parents play in the lives of young people while at the same time helping kids live in the world of their peers. Use this TalkSheet to talk about the role of parents and peers in the lives of the young people in your group.

To Introduce the Topic:

Place two chairs facing each other in the front or the middle of the room. Print the word *parent* on a paper and tape it to one of the chairs. Put the word *peer* on another chair. Ask for volunteers to come up and take turns sitting in the chairs. Tell the group that each chair represents either a parent or a peer perspective. The perspectives could be the same or different, depending upon the issue. Give each volunteer a topic that he or she must debate from both a parent and a peer viewpoint. The volunteer should sit in the proper chair when taking a parent or a peer point of view. Some sample topics are curfew, getting grounded, church attendance, homework, rock music, and chores.

The Discussion:

Item #1: Rebellion is a myth. Most young people get along well with their parents. What families experience are periodic problems or concerns, but constant conflict and rebellion are not normal behavior. Point out that being a teenager does not mean one *has* to rebel.

Item #2: Let kids share their answers with reasons for their responses.

Item #3: This activity is a barometer of the young people's relationships with their parents. It is normal for young adolescents to feel more comfortable talking about certain things with their peers. In fact, some parents try too hard to be their child's friend, leading to an unhealthy relationship. Ask the group to formulate a basic summary statement about this issue. For example, the more important and long-ranging the issue, the more likely the young person will be influenced by parents. Or the older one gets, the more likely she or he is to listen to peers over parents.

Item #4: Ask the students what role they feel their parents should play in their lives. Then ask how they can help their parents best fulfill that role. Point out that parents do need to have a place in their lives. Most parents are not going to abandon their kids to the peer group.

Item #5: Place the headings "Good Stuff" and "Not So Good Stuff" on a chalkboard or on newsprint. Under each, place the passages as kids tell you their appropriate position. Ask for several volunteers to summarize what was learned from this activity.

GOOD STUFF	NOT SO GOOD STUFF
Genesis 13:18	Genesis 13:12, 13
2 Kings 17:28	2 Kings 17:34
Psalm 1:1, 2	Psalm 1:4, 5
Proverbs 1:7-9	Proverbs 1:10-16

To Close the Session:

Tell the group members that they live in two worlds. On the one hand there are their parents with all these expectations, demands, hopes, and plans for them. On the other there is the peer group that also has expectations, demands, hopes, and plans for them. Balancing these two worlds can sometimes seem impossible. That is where their Christian faith can help. Explain that God is not against their friends or their parents. He has offered some guidelines in the Bible related to influences. These are not killjoy principles but a road map to guide you. Read Proverbs 1:8-19 and tell the group that this is only one guideline that must be balanced with others. Generally speaking, for the important things in life you can rely on your parents and must weigh carefully what your friends say. At other times and in some family situations, parents' advice is shakier than that of friends. God's advice and the help of trustworthy Christians are always available. Point out the normalcy of their being comfortable with peers. Most people are more open with their peers—and that includes their parents.

Outside Activity:

There will be a number of situations that are brought up as illustrations during your TalkSheet discussion. Write four or five of these down and ask the group to take them home. Have them ask for their parents' input, write it down, and bring it back to the group to compare notes. The kids will be amazed at the similarity in the parental responses.

TAKING CARE OF BUSINESS

1 What is the first thing you think of when you hear the word *responsibility*?

_____

_____

_____

2 Your opinion, please: **YES, NO,** or **SOMETIMES.**

	YES	NO	SOMETIMES
a. Being responsible is boring.	___	___	___
b. Young people do not need to be responsible.	___	___	___
c. Young people are less responsible than adults.	___	___	___
d. Young people do not get a chance to demonstrate that they can be responsible.	___	___	___
e. Being responsible is part of growing up.	___	___	___

3 Underline the three top reasons you believe average teenagers would give for their irresponsibility.

I'm too young.
I forgot.
There was not enough time.
I'm lazy.
I always have bad luck.
Being responsible is boring.

It was someone else's fault.
I was mad.
I didn't know any better.
I couldn't control myself.
I've never learned to be responsible.
I don't feel like I can be responsible.

4 Circle all the things listed below for which you take responsibility.

Homework
Attending church on your own
Telling the truth
Choosing good friends
Controlling your temper
Not having to be reminded to do something

Chores
Eating right
Obeying school rules
Reading the Bible
Keeping a secret for a friend
Brushing your teeth

5 Look up the following Scriptures and decide which ones describe acting responsibly and which ones describe acting irresponsibly.

Genesis 3:12   **Exodus 32:21-24**   **Psalm 119:1-3**   **Matthew 25:44-46**
Luke 10:33-37   **Luke 15:11-16**   **1 Corinthians 10:33**

TAKING CARE OF BUSINESS
Topic: Responsibility

Purpose of this Session:

Responsibility—young teens say they can handle it. Adults question what teenagers do with it. This all-important growing-up issue can be discussed using this TalkSheet.

To Introduce the Topic:

Walk into the room with strings tied on every finger. Tell the group you are quite forgetful but have turned over a new, responsible leaf. Each string represents something you must remember. Go through each finger and tell what each string will help you remember. You can make these funny by saying things like, "This string reminds me I have to change underwear next week. And this one is a reminder that I have to take out the trash."

Another method to introduce the topic would be to ask your group members to sit in a circle (or circles, if you have a large group). With the room darkened, have one person shine a flashlight (the spotlight) on another's face and fire off questions about responsibility. Only the person in the spotlight may speak. This will focus everyone's attention on the one sharing. The questions can be as deep or as shallow as you wish, and no one is required to answer if he or she is uncomfortable. To begin with, ask questions such as "Do you make your bed?" "How messy is your room?" and "How often have you turned in your homework late?" Do not pass judgment on what is shared. After several have answered, turn the lights back on and announce you will be discussing responsibility.

The Discussion:

Item #1: Let kids share their feelings about the word *responsibility*. Ask the group to come up with a definition of responsibility.

Item #2: Let the young people share their opinions about responsibility. Young people want to be treated as if they are responsible *sometimes*, but they do not always want adult responsibility. They want to decide when they get to be responsible and when they get to be irresponsible. Point out the inconsistency of this kind of thinking.

Item #3: Discuss why so many people, not just teenagers, act in irresponsible ways.

Item #4: Ask the kids why they act responsibly in the areas they circled.

Item #5: Have the young people report their findings on these verses. Ask them to relate what they learned about responsibility. The following are examples of acting responsibly: Psalm 119:1-3, Luke 10:33-37, and 1 Corinthians 10:33. These are examples of acting irresponsibly: Genesis 3:12, Exodus 32:21-24, Matthew 25:44-46, and Luke 15:11-16.

To Close the Session:

Explain to the group that part of our sinful heritage is blaming others rather than taking responsibility. "It's not my fault" thinking began in the garden with Adam and Eve and remains with us today. Examples of no-fault thinking abound in the adult world. The church board blames the pastor for financial problems, the student blames the teacher for a bad grade, the manager blames the worker for lower productivity, and the parent blames the child for acting up. Point out to the group that shirking responsibility is a widespread phenomenon. Rich nations do not want to take responsibility for starving ones. Warring nations blame each other for their problems.

Responsibility is a matter of perspective. Adults are concerned about teenagers and irresponsibility because they know that in the future acting irresponsibly will not be in the teenager's best interest. Teenagers see responsibility a little differently than adults. They believe they are acting responsibly with respect to their futures and their futures are tomorrow or tonight. Responsibility is also seen by teenagers as part of growing up and teenagers do want to grow up. What they see adults do they define as maturity, so kids think that drinking and sex make them grown-up. They have confused adult irresponsibility with maturity.

Outside Activity:

Ask parents to attend a panel and answer questions about responsibility from the young people. Focus on how young people are never going to be responsible if they are not given responsibility.

WOULD YA, SHOULD YA, COULD YA

1 What would our society be like if no one followed the Ten Commandments?

_____

_____

2 Decide which of the following are right and which are wrong.

	THE RIGHT THING TO DO	THE WRONG THING TO DO
a. Lying to a parent.	_____	_____
b. Copying someone else's homework once.	_____	_____
c. Watching R-rated movies.	_____	_____
d. Looking at a pornographic magazine.	_____	_____
e. Talking back to a teacher.	_____	_____
f. Making a joke about a handicapped kid.	_____	_____
g. Forgetting to call your parents to tell them where you are.	_____	_____
h. Putting someone down.	_____	_____
i. Buying more clothes than you need.	_____	_____
j. Reading the Bible once a month.	_____	_____
k. Having a friend your parents disapprove of.	_____	_____

3 When do you feel you have the most difficult time telling right from wrong?

_____

_____

4 Read the following Scriptures and summarize the moral standard in five words or less.

Psalm 34:14 _____

Proverbs 12:13 _____

Proverbs 28:13 _____

Matthew 7:12 _____

Romans 12:9 _____

Romans 12:17 _____

1 John 4:11 _____

WOULD YA, SHOULD YA, COULD YA?
Topic: Morality

Purpose of this Session:

As a concept, morality has blurred and varied meanings to today's adolescents. What is right and what is wrong has become distorted and convoluted. Parents and the church must become more intentional in teaching values and moral standards. This TalkSheet offers you just that opportunity.

To Introduce the Topic:

Borrow some interconnecting building blocks from the children's department of your church. In front of the group build a structure without using any plan. At the same time have someone else build a structure that is well planned. Ask the group to make some observations about the two structures. Ask which one will stand up the longest. Of course, the planned structure will fare better. Compare the building of the two structures to living a life following God's laws versus the world's.

The Discussion:

Item #1: Talk about why God gave us commandments. Ask the question, "Were they to make our lives miserable or were they given because this is the best way to live our lives?" Explore why more and more people are living contrary to God's way and the present and future consequences of doing so.

Item #2: These situations force kids into making moral choices. Ask them how they decided what was right and what was wrong. Were God's standards reflected in their decisions?

Item #3: Take the time to discuss peer pressure and its influence upon individual morality.

Item #4: Each of the passages is a command of God's. Talk about how God's morality, if lived out, is better than the world's morality.

To Close the Session:

Explain that the moral decisions the young people face will grow more difficult and uncertain as they grow older. They will need a moral foundation upon which to base each of these decisions. In the past, society shared a clear standard of right and wrong that was taught to each generation. Today, however, the individual sets his or her own standard. Clear standards are now blurred. But the Christian still has a clear standard in God's word, the Bible. And God has given standards to live by, that if followed will be good for us.

Outside Activity:

Ask the kids to record how many of the Ten Commandments are broken in the next TV program they watch. The next time the group gets together, individuals can share their findings and discuss the implications of societal disregard for God's morality.

STUFF

1

Compared with most other young people at my school, I have . . .

___ better stuff than they do.
___ about the same kind of stuff as they do.
___ not as good of stuff as they do.

2

Circle each of the following things young teenagers should be allowed to personally own.

Color television

Telephone

Latest style shoes

Computer

High-quality bicycle

Video game equipment

CD player or other stereo equipment

Telephone answering machine

Latest style clothing

Workout equipment

Recreational vehicle (motorcycle, Jet Ski, snowmobile, all-terrain vehicle)

VCR

3

Go back to Item #2 and cross out each thing you personally own. Put a star by the things you plan to own by the time you graduate from high school.

4

Suppose you were given a lot of money today. Check (✓) your top two choices of how you would spend that money.

___ Buy lots of things for myself.
___ Use it to help others.
___ Help my family.
___ Give it to the church and missionaries.
___ Save much of it for my future education.
___ Have a good time with my friends.

5

AGREE or **DISAGREE?** Write **A** or **D** beside each statement.

_____ a. A person can have too many possessions.
_____ b. The more one gets, the less one wants.
_____ c. Owning too many material possessions makes it difficult to live the Christian life.
_____ d. Material possessions can make a person popular.
_____ e. Having enough money will be a number one future worry for today's teenagers.

6

Read the following Scriptures and write what you think each has to say about money and possessions.

Exodus 20:17 _____

Matthew 6:24 _____

Luke 12:15 _____

Luke 14:33 _____

STUFF

Topic: The Consumption Expectations of Young Teenagers

Purpose of this Session:

The consumption aspirations and patterns of our general society have adversely affected young people. The mass media seem to profoundly influence the consumption expectations of young people more than the family, the traditional purveyor of values. Whether they are poor, middle class, or rich, kids report high levels of present and future expected consumption of material goods. But are these consumption patterns Christian? This TalkSheet explores the topic of possessions and consumption expectations held by young people.

To Introduce the Topic:

Bring a stack of ads from the Sunday paper. Break the group of young people into clusters of three to five. Ask them to cut out stuff from the ads that they own and stuff that they want to own. They should create two stacks of stuff—things they have and things they want to have. Ask the groups to compare which stack is bigger. Then talk about why they need the stuff they want to have.

Another introductory activity that can be fun is the "Personal Possessions" game. Give each person a piece of paper and something to write with. Have the kids make a list of all the stuff they have on their bodies. They should list all that they are wearing, including what is in their wallets, pockets, and purses. You can also have people include things like glasses, contact lenses, and braces. Next to each item they should write down an estimate of how much it costs. They can then calculate a total amount of the worth of what they are wearing. You can use yourself as an example to explain what needs to be done. Add up the individual totals and you may be surprised at the amount of money that has been spent on the group members. Often this amount will be more than the annual incomes of families in Third World countries.

The Discussion:

Item #1: Most kids say they have about the same amount. We tend to believe that we are the same or better off than those around us. Once you have established the amount of stuff the kids have, ask them if all that stuff is necessary.

Item #2: Let the group debate which items kids should be allowed to own versus those they should not. Ask the kids to consider what having all this stuff does for their Christian witness.

Item #3: Here you will get at the kids' consumption expectations. Ask them why they plan to own the things they underlined. Ask how the things they want could get in the way of their relationship with God.

Item #4: Discuss the different priorities the young people identified.

Item #5: Debate the different issues involved in these statements. Ask kids to back up their opinions with Scripture.

Item #6: These passages will challenge the students to rethink their perspectives on consumption and possessions. Divide the students into small groups to decide what each of these Scriptures has to say about possessions.

To Close the Session:

Today, we consume more and more. But God's kingdom turns things around. God says you must give to get; you must lose your life to save it. Christ repeatedly warned his disciples about the dangers of possessions—they get in the way of living life. Christ enjoyed life as he served God. Luke 7:34 suggests that the Pharisees felt maybe he was enjoying it too much. It was not enjoyment or happiness that Jesus warned us against but the belief that our possessions will provide that happiness. It is our attitude toward stuff that gets us into trouble. Consider the parable of the sower found in Matthew 13 (see verse 22).

Outside Activity:

Ask the kids to examine all the stuff they have and give some of it away to those in need—and not just the stuff they do not want. That is not sacrifice!

SOLUTION SOURCE

1 List three problems that young teenagers commonly face.

a. _____

b. _____

c. _____

2 **AGREE** or **DISAGREE?** Write **A** or **D** beside each statement.

___ **a.** It is easier for Christians to solve their problems than it is for people who are not Christians.

___ **b.** Christian young people have more problems than young people who are not Christians.

___ **c.** Adults don't understand the problems young people face today.

___ **d.** God cares about only the big problems in my life.

___ **e.** I have adults in my life that I can talk to about problems I face.

___ **f.** Young people must find their own solutions to the problems they encounter in life.

3 My Christian beliefs help me make the right choice when I face a problem.

___ **All of the time**

___ **Most of the time**

___ **Some of the time**

___ **None of the time**

4 Read the following Scriptures and write out what you think each has to say about solving problems.

Psalm 34:19 _____

_____

Psalm 120:1 _____

_____

Romans 8:28 _____

_____

James 1:2-5 _____

_____

SOLUTION SOURCE
Topic: Problem Solving and the Christian

Purpose of this Session:

Young adolescents faced with problems often freeze. They are not sure where to turn or what to do. This TalkSheet provides the opportunity to discuss different perspectives on problem solving and how a Christian young person can approach a problem.

To Introduce the Topic:

Give the group one or more sticks of gum (depending upon the size of your group) and announce that you have gum but not enough for everyone to receive a whole piece. Make sure you limit the amount so that the group is faced with a problem-to-be-solved dilemma. Give the available gum to a few individuals and let the group decide what to do. When the group has finally determined a course of action, tell them you want to spend this TalkSheet discussion time on problem solving.

The Discussion:

Item #1: Make a master list of all the reported problems. Ask which ones they think are the worst and why they think these problems are so common. Try to reach a consensus on the top three problems.

Item #2: Call for a vote on the statements. If there is disagreement, discuss the issue with the group. Ask the young people to explain why they agree or disagree. You will need to be prepared to give your own views in response to some of the questions raised. Allow enough time for any questions they might have.

Item #3: Discuss how we as Christians can incorporate our Christian beliefs to help us with the choices we face.

Item #4: Give opportunities for different kids to share their perspectives on the passages. As a group, decide how God wants young people to face the problems they encounter.

To Close the Session:

Generally speaking, God is our partner in problem solving. A biblical case can be made for deferring all our problems to God, but most Christians would probably agree that God and his people together work through their issues. He guides and enables us to solve the problems of living. Emphasize that God is available to help in solving the problems young people face. But we must ask for his help and be willing to listen when he speaks. That means we must have a relationship with God and God's people so that we can discern what God wants for us. Point out that for a partnership to be formed with God we must *live* our Christian beliefs not just *use* our Christianity when we encounter a problem.

Outside Activity:

Ask the kids to write down typical problems they face. Keep this process anonymous. Collect the problems and read them individually to the group. Screen them for appropriateness before you read them out loud. Ask the group to brainstorm solutions to the problems and how God can help in the solutions.

TUNED IN

1

a. How many young people at your school know their astrological signs?
(Place a check mark on one of the lines below to indicate your answer.)

b. How many young people at your school believe in psychic powers like ESP,
spirit contact with the dead, or magic? (Underline your answer on one of the lines below.)

c. How many young people at your school wear crystals? (Circle your answer below.)

___ **Everyone**
___ **Almost everyone**
___ **Some people**
___ **A few people**
___ **Nobody**

2

Write down the name of one movie you have seen where there was contact with spirits or ghosts.

_____

3

Check (✓) each of the ways you believe God reveals himself to us. (You can check more than one.)

_____ God reveals himself through astrology.
_____ God has revealed himself through his Son, Jesus Christ.
_____ God reveals himself through spirit guides.
_____ God reveals himself through contacting the inner self.
_____ God has revealed himself through his written Word, the Bible.
_____ God reveals himself through the calling up of magical forces.
_____ God reveals himself through the power of crystals.
_____ God has revealed himself through his creation.

4

I would like to learn more about what the Bible teaches about . . . (Circle your top two choices.)

The new age movement
Reincarnation
Astrology
Satanism
Crystal power
Other (please specify): _____

5

Read **Deuteronomy 18:9-15** and write what you think is the main message God wants to teach us today
from this passage.

_____
_____
_____
_____
_____

TUNED IN
Topic: Counterfeit Spiritual Guidance

Purpose of this Session:

Young teens encounter crystals, horoscopes, Indian religions, and Eastern meditation techniques at school, with their friends, and through contact with the mass media. Take this opportunity to talk about these spiritual counterfeits with your group through a TalkSheet discussion.

To Introduce the Topic:

For this introduction you will need a tire air pressure gauge and a Bible. Hold up both the tire gauge and the Bible, and ask the group how a Bible is similar to a tire gauge. What can each test? Explain that as a tire gauge is used to test air pressure, the Bible is used to test truth. How often should each be used? How accurate are each of these? Explain to your group that the Bible is an accurate gauge that can be used to measure the truth of spiritual teachings and beliefs. And today there is so much counterfeit spiritual information that somehow there needs to be a gauge to test its validity. Tell the group that the discussion will revolve around spiritual counterfeit guidance and what to do with it. Then pass out the TalkSheets.

You can also introduce the topic with the game "Squeak, Bunny, Squeak." Seat everyone in a circle of chairs. One person is chosen to be "It" and must stand blindfolded and holding a pillow in the middle of the circle. While the leader spins "It" around twice, the players seated in the circle change chairs. "It" must now locate a person, place the pillow on that person's lap, sit on it, and say, "Squeak, bunny, squeak." The person who is being sat on disguises his or her voice and squeaks while "It" tries to guess whose lap it is. If the guess is correct, the person who is identified becomes the new "It." After a few minutes of play, discuss how spiritual deceivers attempt to delude us through disguising the truth just as we tried to fake our voices.

The Discussion:

Item #1: This item gives you an indicator of the level of spiritual counterfeit activity occurring at local schools. Take a poll of the group's responses. Ask the group why people would believe it is important to know their astrological signs? To believe in magic spiritual forces? To wear a crystal?

Item #2: Make a list of recent movies with spiritual counterfeit content. Ask the group how these movies influence people in subtle and not so subtle ways.

Item #3: The following are ways in which God reveals himself: God has revealed himself through his Son, Jesus Christ; God has revealed himself through his written Word, the Bible; and God has revealed himself through his creation.

Item #4: Check out the interest level of your group to further explore the resurgence in spiritual counterfeit movements. If interest is high, you will want to pursue it within your Christian education format.

Item #5: Let a number of kids share their thoughts on how this passage applies to us today.

To Close the Session:

Explain to the group that wanting guidance is a normal part of life and growing up. We all want to know what is in store for us. The children of Israel continuously sought guidance—sometimes from God and other times from false gods and spiritual mediums. God has promised to guide those who follow him (Psalm 31:3). Each of us has access to the infinite yet personal God of the Bible who wants the best for us. We have no need to turn to counterfeit advice with its false promises. Close by reading Hebrews 13:9.

Outside Activity:

You can obtain additional information for your group to study regarding the issues raised by writing to: Spiritual Counterfeit Projects, P.O. Box 4308, Berkeley, CA 94704.

WHAT PLACE WILL CHRIST TAKE?

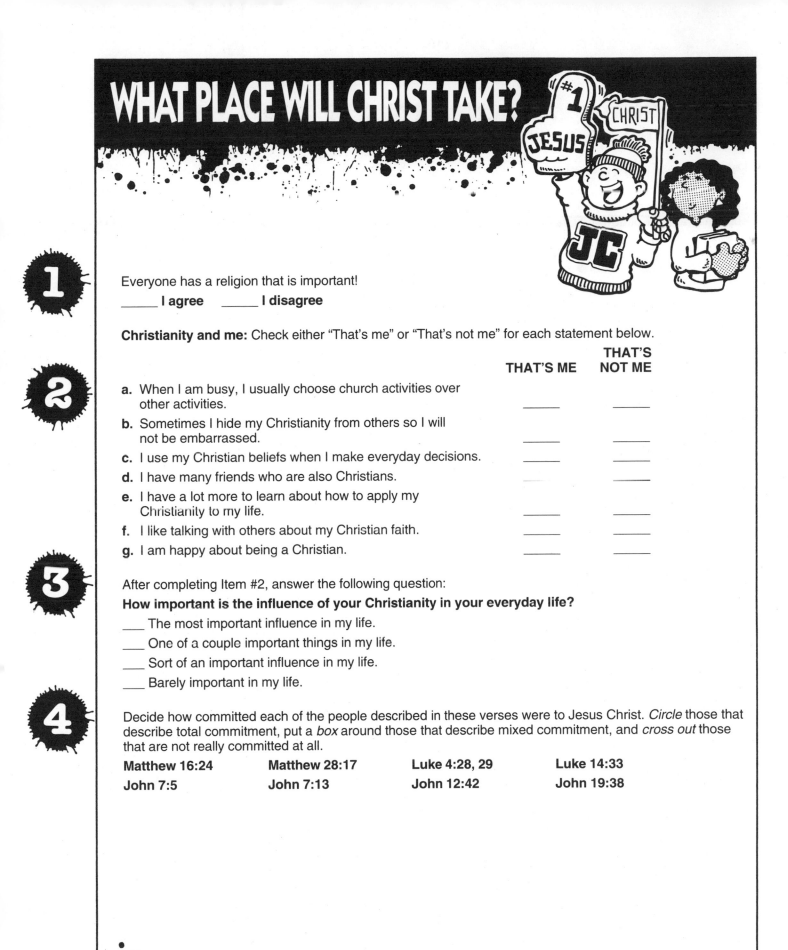

1 Everyone has a religion that is important!

_____ **I agree**   _____ **I disagree**

2 **Christianity and me:** Check either "That's me" or "That's not me" for each statement below.

	THAT'S ME	THAT'S NOT ME
a. When I am busy, I usually choose church activities over other activities.	_____	_____
b. Sometimes I hide my Christianity from others so I will not be embarrassed.	_____	_____
c. I use my Christian beliefs when I make everyday decisions.	_____	_____
d. I have many friends who are also Christians.	_____	_____
e. I have a lot more to learn about how to apply my Christianity to my life.	_____	_____
f. I like talking with others about my Christian faith.	_____	_____
g. I am happy about being a Christian.	_____	_____

3 After completing Item #2, answer the following question:

How important is the influence of your Christianity in your everyday life?

___ The most important influence in my life.

___ One of a couple important things in my life.

___ Sort of an important influence in my life.

___ Barely important in my life.

4 Decide how committed each of the people described in these verses were to Jesus Christ. *Circle* those that describe total commitment, put a *box* around those that describe mixed commitment, and *cross out* those that are not really committed at all.

Matthew 16:24	**Matthew 28:17**	**Luke 4:28, 29**	**Luke 14:33**
John 7:5	**John 7:13**	**John 12:42**	**John 19:38**

WHAT PLACE WILL CHRIST TAKE?
Topic: The Importance of One's Christianity

Purpose of this Session:

Young Christian teenagers, if they have not already done so, are about to come to a fork in the spiritual road. When they were younger they attended church, prayed, and memorized Bible verses because that was what they were supposed to do. But now they have a choice. What importance will Christianity take during their adolescence? Use this TalkSheet opportunity to talk about the role of Christianity in the lives of your young people.

To Introduce the Topic:

You will need a television programming guide for this activity. Tell your kids that they are going to be quizzed on a subject most of them know very well. Using the television guide as your reference, ask the group questions like, "What is on at seven p.m. Thursday night on Channel Nine?" Most of the kids will get the questions right, especially if you ask questions covering after-school and prime-time programming. Point out to them that they passed the test because the content was important to them. Then tell the students that the TalkSheet discussion will cover the importance of another issue—their Christianity.

The Discussion:

Item #1: Ask the group to name other religions like Mormonism, Judaism, and Jehovah's Witness. There are also things like sports, music, video games, or skateboarding that can act like other gods.

Item #2: Make a master list and poll the group. The young people may push you to add an in-between column "That's Sort of Me."

Item #3: You could have the group members rank in order their involvement in each of the following as one way to measure their commitment: sports, church stuff, school, goofing around, and friends. You can also use this time to talk about how the youth group can structure itself to help group members become more committed to their Christianity.

Item #4: Take a vote to see where the majority of your group members rank the commitment level of those in the verses. Any disagreement needs to be discussed. Then talk about what the young people learned about commitment to their Christian lives.

To Close the Session:

Use the following questions to wrap up the session. How committed do you want to be to your Christian faith? What kind of relationship do you want to have with Jesus Christ? How many things are more important than God? When God gave the Ten Commandments, he knew that there would be many things that would compete for our attention. This probably explains why the first commandment was first (Exodus 20:3). What crowds out God in your life? Whatever it is, it is your god. You are committed to something! How much of this commitment is directed toward your Christian faith?

Outside Activity:

Have your group create a short survey about the importance of one's Christianity that can be given to adults. Ask each group member to survey three adults. Bring the results to the group, tabulate the results, and make some observations about what was learned about commitment to the Christian faith.

ECO-CHRISTIANS

 Answer the following question:
What does *away* mean when you throw something away?

_____

_____

_____

 Most students at my school . . . (Circle only one.)

a. do not care about environmental problems.

b. care about environmental problems but do not do much about them.

c. care about environmental problems and do something about them.

 Your opinion, please: **YES, NO,** or **MAYBE SO.**

	YES	NO	MAYBE
a. God cares about the environment.	___	___	___
b. The Bible offers some practical solutions for today's environmental problems.	___	___	___
c. There is a real Mother Earth.	___	___	___
d. Problems with the environment are a sign it is the last days before Christ's return.	___	___	___
e. The environmental abuses of today will be taken care of by the time you are an adult.	___	___	___

 What is one thing your church could do to be a better steward of the world God created?

_____

_____

_____

 Read **Psalm 8** and decide what this says to Christians about the environment.

ECO-CHRISTIANS
Topic: Christians and the Environment

Purpose of this Session:

Environmental issues have been neglected by the church. Consequently, many young teenagers have little idea about a Christian view of ecology. The new age movement is making substantial inroads in promoting its worldview using the issue of the environment as an evangelistic tool. Take this opportunity to talk about a Christian perspective on the environment.

To Introduce the Topic:

Place the following environmental issues on the chalkboard or on newsprint and ask volunteers to define the problem for each.

Species extinction	**Natural resources depletion**	**Garbage overload**
Acid rain	**Greenhouse effect**	**Water pollution**
Hazardous waste	**Ozone depletion**	**Air pollution**
Littering	**Rain forest destruction**	

Another introductory activity would be to litter the room with pop cans and other household trash that is safe. When the young people arrive for your group meeting, keep the litter on the floor to use as an illustration during the discussion. Ask the group how it feels to see so much litter scattered around the room. Did the kids feel any responsibility to pick up the litter?

The Discussion:

Item #1: Use this question to discuss our relationship with the environment.

Item #2: Take a poll of the group members to see where their schools stand in relationship to the environment.

Item #3: These statements give you an opportunity to talk about a proper Christian perspective on ecology and the environment.

Item #4: Brainstorm a list of ideas, then ask the students what they want to do with the list. Kids may want to make this an outside project so they can do additional research.

Item #5: Discuss the awesome responsibility we have been given by God to take care of his creation. Ask the group how it thinks God feels about the kind of job Christians have been doing taking care of his creation.

To Close the Session:

The new age movement seeks to bring Eastern thinking to the West. New agers seek to elevate the animal, plant, and mineral world to the level of human beings. They see all things as an undifferentiated oneness, a worldview called *monism*. The wish to elevate this oneness to the level of deity creates the pantheistic view that all is one, all is god. And because all is divine, all should be treated equally. In India, people are starving because food is given to cows and rats. In contrast to this, the Bible teaches that people are created in God's image (Genesis 1:26). This gives people value, not as the new agers contend because they are god, but because in fact they are God's creation. People are uniquely divided from the animal, plant, and mineral world. Yet, people are united with that world because all of it was created by God. Because God created everything—the animal, plant, and mineral world as well as mankind—everything has value (Leviticus 25:23; 1 Chronicles 29:14-16; Psalm 50:10, 11; and Haggai 2:8). It is this Christian view of creation that gives creation its meaning. Because God created animals, plants, oceans, and mountains, they are worth respecting. It has been a distorted interpretation of Genesis 1:28 that has given us the idea that the world and all it contains was created for us to exploit. So we have wasted what God intended us to treat with respect. He created us a little lower than the angels and wants us to take care of what he made. We are responsible for creation because of our high position. Sin, however, has separated us from God and has affected creation. The Bible teaches that the whole of creation awaits God's redemption (Romans 8:18-25). While we await God's return to redeem all he made, we are responsible as Christians for what Francis Schaeffer called the "substantial healing" of creation.* We cannot perfect what sin has ruined, but we can go a long way in the healing process.

Outside Activity:

Challenge the group to tackle a project that will help heal God's hurting creation. There are a number of books that have project ideas available at your local library.

* Francis Schaeffer, *Pollution and the Death of Man: The Christian View of Ecology* (Wheaton, Ill.: Tyndale House, 1970).

FAMILY DAZE

1 Describe a time you felt really close to your family.

_____

_____

_____

2 Some families leave notes for each other on their refrigerators. Write out a note you would like to leave your family on your refrigerator.

Dear Family:

_____

_____

_____

_____

_____

3 **You and your family.** After each of the following statements, check either **YES** or **NO**.

	YES, THAT'S MY FAMILY	NO, THAT'S NOT MY FAMILY
a. Family life is as good as it will ever get.	_____	_____
b. Our family sacrifices for each other.	_____	_____
c. Family members cooperate with each other.	_____	_____
d. If there is a problem, our family is able to solve it.	_____	_____
e. Our family is like most other families.	_____	_____
f. Family members are able to talk with each other.	_____	_____
g. The family has fun together.	_____	_____
h. Our family spends the right amount of time together.	_____	_____

4 Are you glad to be a member of your family? (Check one.)

___ **Yes**   ___ **Sometimes**   ___ **No**

5 Decide which passage is the most helpful in dealing with your family life. Circle the Scripture you chose.

Psalm 42:11	**Matthew 18:21, 22**	**Ephesians 4:2**
Psalm 68:5	**Romans 12:12**	**1 John 3:1-3**
Proverbs 11:29	**Galatians 5:22, 23**	**1 John 4:10-12**

FAMILY DAZE
Topic: Family Life

Purpose of this Session:

Family life has undergone enormous changes in recent years. Yet, the family is still the biggest influence and most important institution in the lives of the majority of young people. Take time to discuss this all-important institution with your students.

To Introduce the Topic:

Create artificial families by using yarn to loosely tie together four or five group members at the wrists. You will need two feet of yarn per person. Once these family ties are fastened, give the group members the following assignments. They are to eat a family meal together. This is a candy bar that they are to share together. They are to do a chore together. Assign each group a specific task like taking out the trash, cleaning a bathroom, or vacuuming a rug. They are to take a trip. This could be a simple walk around the church or meeting place. Call the families back together and ask them to share how their meals, chores, and trips went. Cut your family members loose and pass out the TalkSheets. You can refer back to this lead-in experience during your discussion.

The Discussion:

Item #1: You will need a safe climate for kids to share these experiences. Young teenagers are beginning the process of individuation and will not feel comfortable sharing unless they are reasonably sure they will not be put down. Begin by sharing one of your own junior high school experiences of closeness with your family.

Item #2: Let volunteers read their notes. You will get both positive and antagonistic ones. Ask the volunteers to state why they chose to write what they did.

Item #3: Have young people talk about their own families. Remind the group of your confidentiality rule. Facilitate a spirit of Christian support and love. Brainstorm ways group members can build up their families.

Item #4: Do not have kids publicly share their answers. Rather, ask kids what it takes to be a proud member of a family. Let the group members know that you will be available to talk with them privately about their personal concerns related to family life.

Item #5: Ask young people to share the passages they felt were most helpful in dealing with their family lives.

To Close the Session:

Wrap up the discussion by positively affirming the need for family. You can play a vital role in supporting family life by what you say. Form a circle and pray for one another's families.

Outside Activity:

For this activity you will need to develop a "Family Tree" handout for each of your group members. This can be a simple design like the one below.

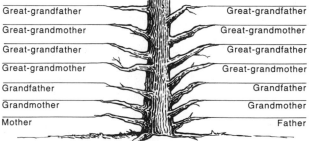

Great-grandfather	Great-grandfather
Great-grandmother	Great-grandmother
Great-grandfather	Great-grandfather
Great-grandmother	Great-grandmother
Grandfather	Grandfather
Grandmother	Grandmother
Mother	Father

Ask the young people to talk with their parents or grandparents to complete their family trees. They are to go as far back as their great-grandparents if they can. It might be fun for your group members to ask questions of some of the family members. The following are possible questions:

1. Did you have a nickname?
2. Who were you named after?
3. What was your dad like?
4. What games did you play growing up?
5. What did your father do for his career?
6. What did your grandmother look like?

Your group members may have some great questions of their own. Have them report any interesting findings back to the group.

PRIORITY PUZZLE

1 Answer the following question: **What is the absolute, number one, biggest, most important first in your life?**

_____

2 Check the **five most important** things in your life right now!

___ Getting homework done on time.
___ Being cool.
___ Watching your favorite TV programs.
___ Wearing the right clothes.
___ Having the right friends.
___ Talking to people about Jesus Christ.
___ Volunteering to help others.
___ Having a boyfriend/girlfriend.

___ Getting money for yourself.
___ Finding out how to get close to God.
___ Being good at a sport.
___ Spending time with your family.
___ Participating in church activities.
___ Having fun.
___ Watching music videos.

3 **TRUE** or **FALSE?**

T   F   Junior high/middle school students do not need to worry about priorities.

T   F   If people let the Bible set their priorities, they will have unhappy lives.

T   F   Adults do a better job at ordering their priorities than teenagers.

T   F   Church does not have to be a priority for someone to live the Christian life.

4 Draw a line connecting the Scriptures with the correct paraphrased Bible statements.

1. Proverbs 3:6   **a. Seek God's priorities and everything else will fall into place.**

2. Matthew 7:21   **b. Obeying Christ's teachings shows our love for him.**

3. Luke 9:23   **c. Recognize God in your priorities and he will make you successful.**

4. Luke 12:31   **d. Not everyone who says God is number one lives like God is number one.**

5. John 14:23   **e. Willingness to do what Christ wants demonstrates our desire to make God number one.**

6. Romans 12:2   **f. Caring about others rather than things should be a top priority for God's people.**

7. 1 Peter 4:8   **g. God wants us to do good, pleasing, and perfect things rather than being like the world.**

PRIORITY PUZZLE
Topic: Priorities

Purpose of this Session:

This TalkSheet takes an honest look at the priorities of young people. In a culture that pulls kids in all directions, take time to help your students see why God needs to be in the center of their lives and priorities.

To Introduce the Topic:

Ask some senior citizens to share their stories with the group. Prep the senior adults to talk about how they might have lived out their lives differently. Let the kids ask them questions about priorities.

A twist on this idea would be to ask high schoolers to attend and share their junior high stories, talking about what they wish they had done differently.

The Discussion:

Item #1: Many kids will tell you what you want to hear. Challenge the students to look at what they like to spend their time doing.

Item #2: Have the group work together to prioritize the five most important things for the group. Then ask the young people to identify the five most important things for kids who are not Christians. Compare and contrast these two lists.

Item #3: As you have the young people reveal their answers to these statements, ask them to reflect on the previous activity of comparing their answers with those of kids who are not Christians.

Item #4: Invite the group to ask questions about the Bible's perspective on priorities. Have individuals share what they learned from the passages. Get practical with ways kids can make God number one in their lives—service to God through service to others, learning more about God, and so on.

To Close the Session:

Point out that priorities can be easy to set but hard to live. Where they need to be set is in our hearts. Matthew 6:21 could be paraphrased to say "For where your priorities are, there your heart will be also." As you daily live your priorities out, they will become etched on your heart. We should look at how we live if we want to really examine our priorities. As Christians we are new creatures called to live new lives.

Outside Activity:

Have the group members keep a "priorities log" that contains all of the big things they did during the week. The young people can bring their logs back to the group and talk about how well they were able to live out their stated priorities.

HOLY MASQUERADE

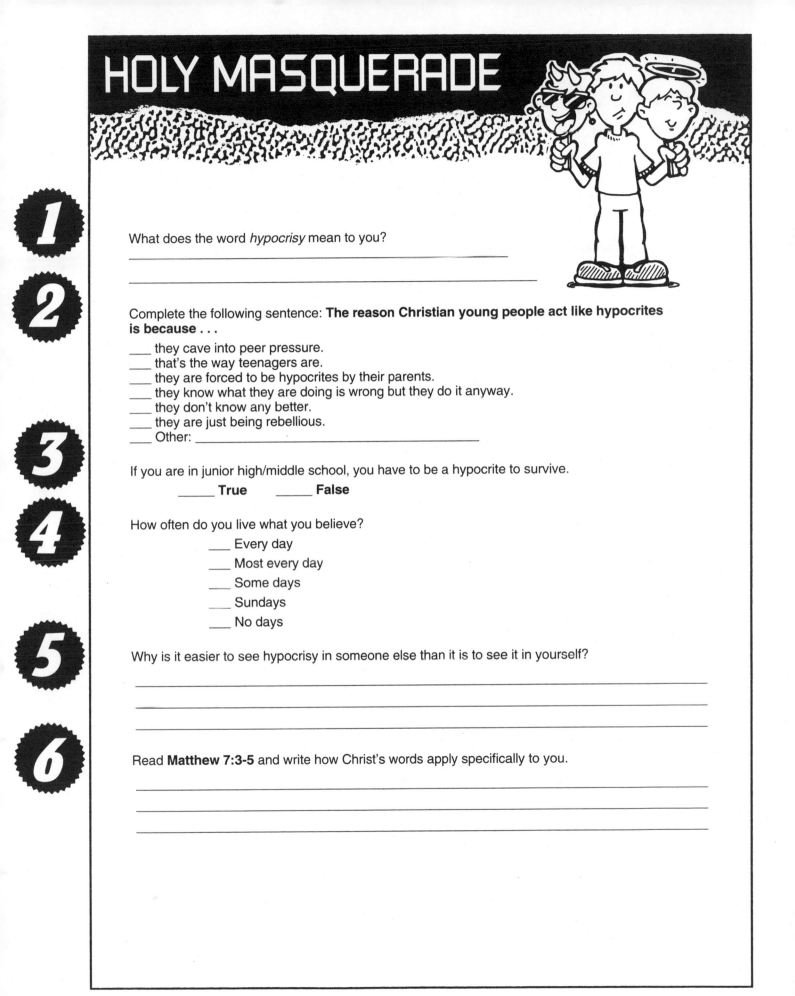

1 What does the word *hypocrisy* mean to you?

_____

_____

2 Complete the following sentence: **The reason Christian young people act like hypocrites is because . . .**

___ they cave into peer pressure.
___ that's the way teenagers are.
___ they are forced to be hypocrites by their parents.
___ they know what they are doing is wrong but they do it anyway.
___ they don't know any better.
___ they are just being rebellious.
___ Other: _____

3 If you are in junior high/middle school, you have to be a hypocrite to survive.

_____ **True**   _____ **False**

4 How often do you live what you believe?

___ Every day
___ Most every day
___ Some days
___ Sundays
___ No days

5 Why is it easier to see hypocrisy in someone else than it is to see it in yourself?

_____

_____

_____

6 Read **Matthew 7:3-5** and write how Christ's words apply specifically to you.

_____

_____

_____

HOLY MASQUERADE
Topic: The Problem of Personal Hypocrisy

Purpose of this Session:

Take this opportunity to discuss with your group of young people the concept of practicing what they preach. You will need to be sensitive to the spiritual condition of the individuals involved in your group. A heavy hand will not force your kids to live their Christian faith. In fact, an authoritarian style may push kids toward further hypocrisy. Keep the discussion honest and open for the best results.

To Introduce the Topic:

Use the Halloween tradition to introduce this two-faced topic. Bring in several Halloween masks to the group. Have several kids come forward and try on the masks. Talk about how pranks are pulled on Halloween because people's identities are hidden. People pretend to be someone they are not and get away with things they normally would not do. Hypocrisy is like wearing a Halloween mask. You pretend you are somebody you really are not and you think you are getting away with something.

The Discussion:

Item #1: Construct a group definition of *hypocrisy*. Write it in a place where everyone can see it so you can refer to it later in the discussion.

Item #2: Poll the group to get the two or three biggest reasons Christian young people act like hypocrites.

Item #3: Discuss hypocrisy as a survival skill. How much of a reality is this for the members of your group? What are other alternatives to hypocrisy to survive junior high/middle school?

Item #4: This gives young people an opportunity to examine how consistently they practice what they preach.

Item #5: Let different group members share their opinions. Ask the group how it can better identify its own hypocrisy rather than judging others.

Item #6: There must be a high level of safety within the group if you choose to ask volunteers to share what they wrote. If you choose not to ask for volunteers, give an example from your own life.

To Close the Session:

One way to look at hypocrisy is to view it as the opposite of repentance. Instead of realizing a sin and confessing it, a hypocrite pretends to not be in need of repentance. The hypocrite goes through the Christian motions for the purpose of fooling others or perhaps himself or herself. Young people need to realize that all of us are hypocrites to one degree or another. We are hypocrites every time we judge another (Matthew 7:1). We are hypocrites every time we talk about our sin in the past tense (1 John 1:8). Adults are usually quick to point out the hypocrisy of youths while youths are quick to point out that adults do not practice what they preach. The Bible warns against being deceived by sin, which gives birth to hypocrisy (Romans 7:11; Jeremiah 17:9; and 1 Corinthians 3:18).

Outside Activity:

Ask several of the students to study hypocrisy throughout the Bible and make a report to the group. They can use a study tool like *Nave's Topical Bible* to help guide their work.

SEX IS NOT A FOUR-LETTER WORD

1 Circle the words below that best describe how you feel about sex.

Scared	Godly	Pleasurable
Moral	Sinful	Good
Confused	Excited	Hurtful
Perverted	Excellent	Sick
Fantastic	Disgusted	Unbelievable
Weird	Sanctified	Strange

2 a. Why is sex not a four-letter word?_____

b. When can sex become a four-letter word?_____

3 Decide what most people at your school think for each of the statements.

a. **It is not a good thing to be a virgin in high school.**
   ___ Most people at my school would say this is true.
   ___ Most people at my school would say this is not true.

b. **It is more okay for a boy to have sex than a girl.**
   ___ Most people at my school would say this is true.
   ___ Most people at my school would say this is not true.

c. **Teenagers cannot be stopped from having sex.**
   ___ Most people at my school would say this is true.
   ___ Most people at my school would say this is not true.

4 Your opinion, please!

	GOOD REASON TO SAY NO TO SEX	DUMB REASON TO SAY NO TO SEX
a. You might get a sexually transmitted disease.	_____	_____
b. Your parents might find out.	_____	_____
c. You want to keep a good reputation.	_____	_____
d. So sex will be the best when you get married.	_____	_____
e. Because it would be wrong.	_____	_____
f. So you could keep your friends.	_____	_____
g. You may not love the person.	_____	_____
h. You don't know how to have sex.	_____	_____
i. Because God wants you to wait until you are married.	_____	_____
j. You're too young to be a parent.	_____	_____
k. Because sex is not good for you.	_____	_____
l. Sex before marriage can hurt a relationship.	_____	_____
m. Because you are afraid.	_____	_____

5 Read each of the Bible verses and finish the sentences accordingly.

The world says premarital sex is okay for teenagers, but the Bible says . . .

(1 Corinthians 6:18-20) _____
The world says that being a virgin is not a good thing, but the Bible says . . .

(1 Thessalonians 4:3-8) _____
The world says God is a no fun, sexual party pooper, but the Bible says . . .

(Proverbs 5:18, 19) _____
The world says premarital sex gives you freedom in a relationship, but the Bible says . . .

(Romans 7:4-6) _____

SEX IS NOT A FOUR-LETTER WORD
Topic: Premarital Sex

Purpose of this Session:

The young people of today are constantly bombarded with the message that premarital sex is acceptable. They need to hear the other side of the story in a positive, nonjudgmental way. This TalkSheet offers the opportunity to discuss sexuality in a Christian context. It is possible to explain that premarital sex is wrong without having to lecture and preach. You may want to consider separating the boys and the girls for the discussion, then bringing them together for a process time and wrap-up. While separated, the boys and the girls can think of some questions they have for the opposite sex.

To Introduce the Topic:

Ask one of the young people to bring a model car or plane she or he has assembled and one not yet assembled with the assembly directions. Use these two as illustrations to demonstrate how well the assembled model looks because Jason or Jennifer followed directions. Ask the group to guess what the unassembled model might look like if you began putting it together without following the directions. Tell the group that a person's sex life is like these models—it can be great if God's directions are followed, but a mess if they are ignored.

The Discussion:

Item #1: Before letting the group members share their circled responses, go over the ground rules found on page 12. Obtain a group consensus about how kids feel about sex. This can set a positive, mature tone to the discussion. Allow kids to share both the positive and negative words. You can summarize by saying sex can be viewed in both positive and negative ways depending upon attitudes and behaviors. Be sensitive to the variety of perspectives suggested. Some of the young people in your group will have already had bad experiences such as molestation or premarital sex.

Item #2: Let the group tackle both of the questions before providing any of your own answers. Describe God's intentions for sex—to reserve sex for marriage since that is the best, most loving, and fun relationship for sex. Give some examples of how sex becomes a four-letter word—molestation, rape, and exploitive sex, such as premarital sex.

Item #3: Here you will be able to gauge the kids' sexual attitudes that shape their present and future sexual behaviors. After letting the group members share their opinions of their peers at school, engage them in sharing their own views. Begin sharing what God might have to say about virginity, the double standard, and controlling sexual urges.

Item #4: You now have a chance to provide some solid reasons for abstinence. It is important for you to let the kids see both the good and the dumb reasons to wait. Many kids will hear mostly dumb reasons to wait and thus go ahead and have premarital sex. Let them hear some of the smart reasons as well.

Item #5: Make a list of the differences between what the prevailing societal standard is versus what God has to say about sex. Ask the group to decide which standard makes the most sense and why.

To Close the Session:

Summarize the points that have been covered. Reflect on the introductory activity reminding the group that you needed to follow the model's directions to ensure its proper assembly. For our sexual lives to be the best, we need to follow God's sexual directions given to us in the Bible. Emphasize your willingness to talk to them about sexual topics they may need to discuss privately and confidentially (sexual abuse, abortion, sexual mistakes, and so on). Explain that God gave these directions in the Bible not because he wanted us to live dull, uneventful lives, but because these are the best way to live life. Close by reading 1 Thessalonians 4:1-8.

Outside Activity:

It is imperative for parents and young people to communicate about sex. Ask your students to interview their parents on the subject. If someone feels it is impossible to talk to a parent, suggest yourself or another reliable adult. Let them create a list of questions to ask parents and refer to the interview as a youth group assignment that is required.

SATAN, INC.

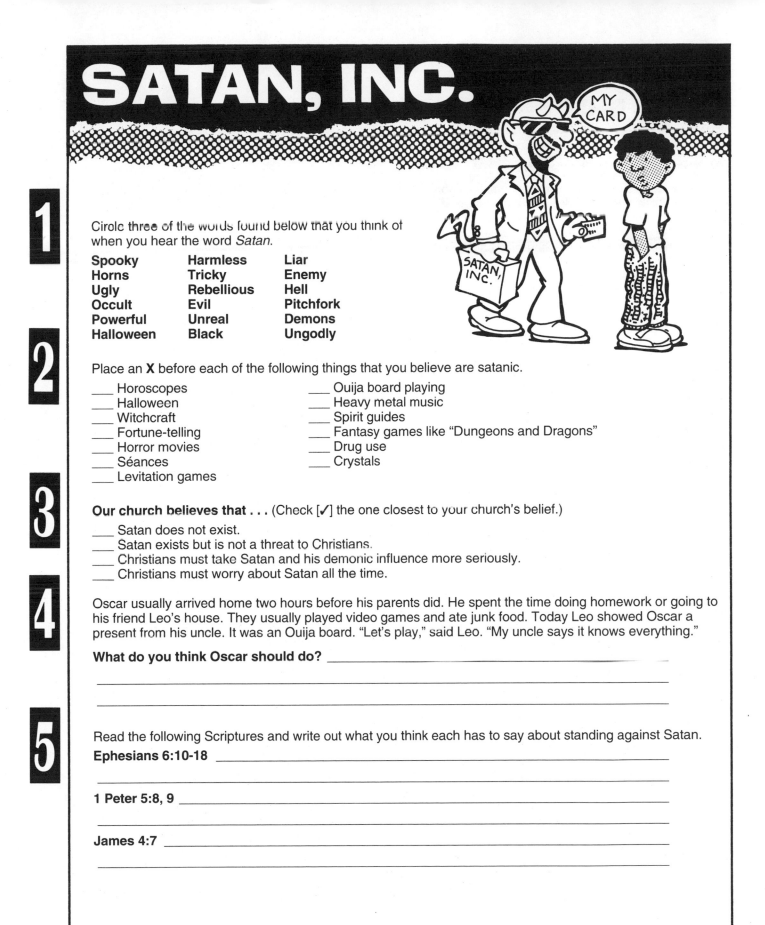

1 Circle three of the words found below that you think of when you hear the word *Satan*.

Spooky	**Harmless**	**Liar**
Horns	**Tricky**	**Enemy**
Ugly	**Rebellious**	**Hell**
Occult	**Evil**	**Pitchfork**
Powerful	**Unreal**	**Demons**
Halloween	**Black**	**Ungodly**

2 Place an **X** before each of the following things that you believe are satanic.

___ Horoscopes   ___ Ouija board playing
___ Halloween   ___ Heavy metal music
___ Witchcraft   ___ Spirit guides
___ Fortune-telling   ___ Fantasy games like "Dungeons and Dragons"
___ Horror movies   ___ Drug use
___ Séances   ___ Crystals
___ Levitation games

3 **Our church believes that . . .** (Check [✓] the one closest to your church's belief.)

___ Satan does not exist.
___ Satan exists but is not a threat to Christians.
___ Christians must take Satan and his demonic influence more seriously.
___ Christians must worry about Satan all the time.

4 Oscar usually arrived home two hours before his parents did. He spent the time doing homework or going to his friend Leo's house. They usually played video games and ate junk food. Today Leo showed Oscar a present from his uncle. It was an Ouija board. "Let's play," said Leo. "My uncle says it knows everything."

What do you think Oscar should do? _____

_____

_____

5 Read the following Scriptures and write out what you think each has to say about standing against Satan.
Ephesians 6:10-18 _____

_____

1 Peter 5:8, 9 _____

_____

James 4:7 _____

_____

Date Used: _____   Group: _____

SATAN, INC.
Topic: Satanism

Purpose of this Session:

C. S. Lewis wrote in *The Screwtape Letters*, "There are two equal and opposite errors into which our race can fall about the devils. One is to disbelieve in their existence. The other is to believe and to feel an excessive and unhealthy interest in them."* It is the intention of this TalkSheet to do neither, yet the tendency has been when talking with people about satanism to err on either side. Too many times talking about the satanic will spark curiosity in kids and they're off to the local library to check out the *Satanic Bible* or other occult literature. The discussion that takes place should not focus upon the gory details of satanic rituals and worship, but we must address the realities of satanic involvement by today's youths. Use this TalkSheet to generate a balanced discussion on the reality of Satan in today's world.

To Introduce the Topic:

One way of quickly introducing this topic is to ask the group members to name all of the movies that contain demonic or satanic themes. You can then point out the growing trend in our culture toward the satanic.

Another way to introduce this topic is through tape recording different people's opinions about satanism. Go to several church members of different ages or people at large in front of a store or a mall and ask what they believe about Satan and the occult. Try to get several differing opinions. Play these for the group after editing them.

The Discussion:

Item #1: Ask the young people to share the words chosen and explain why. State that you would like to discuss satanism and the demonic without acting in an immature manner and without putting others down.

Item #2: Expect a wide variety of responses here. Explain to the group that Satan works through each of the items listed. Satan is called "the father of lies" and he will use anything he can to deceive people.

Item #3: Take the time to explain what your church believes. You may want to have the pastor on hand to help answer questions.

Item #4: Ask the kids how many of them have been tempted or dabbled in satanic things like Ouija boards, tarot cards, and the like. Have the group members brainstorm ways they can "resist the devil."

Item #5: This activity provides you with the opportunity to discuss how Christians can resist and thwart the work of the adversary. Divide the young people into small groups and have each group take a different passage of Scripture. Allow enough time for them to reach a consensus on what they think the passage says about what a Christian's response to the devil should be. Each of the small groups can then report back to the group as a whole.

To Close the Session:

Explain to the group that one of Satan's strategies is to convince people he does not exist. The other strategy is to convince people he is real and can provide them with power. This is appealing to some young people, especially those who feel powerless. But this power is false and empty. Only the one true God has the power for living. Emphasize the reality of Satan and the evil work he and his demons are carrying out in today's world. This can be effectively and quickly done by pointing out some of the names the Bible has given Satan: accuser (Revelation 12:10), enemy (1 Peter 5:8), evil one (1 John 5:19), liar (John 8:44), and tempter (Matthew 4:3). Also emphasize that Christ came to destroy the work of the devil (1 John 3:8), that Christ has rescued us from Satan's power (Colossians 1:18), and that Christ who dwells in every Christian through the Holy Spirit is greater than Satan (1 John 4:4).

Outside Activity:

Have the group search the Scriptures for examples of how biblical characters dealt with Satan.

*C. S. Lewis, *The Screwtape Letters* (New York: Macmillan, 1959 and 1961), Preface.

OPPOSITE SEX BLUES

1 What one word do you feel best describes the opposite sex?

_____

2 Complete the following sentences:

Most girls think boys are . . . _____

_____

Most boys think girls are . . . _____

_____

3 **TRUE or FALSE?**

a. _____ Girls and boys can be best friends.
b. _____ Christians should be together only with other Christians.
c. _____ It is permissible for a girl to ask a boy to go with her.
d. _____ Boys are more committed to Christ than girls.
e. _____ Most junior high/middle school students get into opposite sex relationships because every one else is going together.
f. _____ If your parents don't approve of the person you are seeing, you should stop seeing him or her.
g. _____ A young person your age cannot be in love.
h. _____ Girls want opposite sex relationships more than boys.

4 What advice would you give a friend who was in each of the following situations:

a. Your friend is at a party and people begin playing kissing games. _____

_____

b. Your friend is good friends with a member of the opposite sex and starts liking that person for more than just a friend. _____

c. Your friend is asked out by a member of the opposite sex. _____

_____

d. Your friend is home alone after school and a member of the opposite sex stops by to hang out.

_____

5 If you could have only one question answered about the opposite sex, what would that question be?

_____

6 Match the Scriptures with the statements on the right.

1. **Romans 15:7**   a. **Love each other.**
2. **Galatians 5:13-15**   b. **Pray for each other.**
3. **Ephesians 6:18**   c. **Serve each other.**
4. **1 Thessalonians 5:11** d. **Accept each other.**
5. **1 Peter 1:22**   e. **Encourage each other.**

OPPOSITE SEX BLUES
Topic: Relating to the Opposite Sex

Purpose of this Session:

Young people have many questions and concerns about the opposite sex that often go unanswered. Increasingly they report members of the opposite sex on their friendship lists as they move from grade to grade. They want more contact with the opposite sex but are often not quite sure what to do. Help with the confusion about appropriate relationships with the opposite sex by using this TalkSheet. You can help your kids get answers to their questions and examine their opposite sex relationships from a Christian perspective. (See also "TOGETHER," page 17, and "SEX IS NOT A FOUR-LETTER WORD," page 75.)

To Introduce the Topic:

Play "Spin the Bottle" with a slight twist. Instead of laying a kiss on a random player, the spinner gets to ask whomever the bottle points to at the end of its spin a question about the opposite sex. You can use an empty plastic 32-ounce soda bottle for the spinner.

The Discussion:

Item #1: Have the students share the words they chose and the reasons why. As questions arise about the opposite sex, you can begin a written list on the chalkboard or newsprint. Keep the list running throughout the discussion and have the group answer them at the end of the session. Let adults answer them as well as the young people.

Item #2: Give both sexes their chance to defend their position. It can be fun to sit the boys together and the girls together, but don't let the battle between the sexes get out of hand.

Item #3: Use these statements as a vehicle to discuss the importance of thinking through relationships. Young people at this age often rush into serious romantic opposite sex relationships before they are ready. Emphasize the importance of maintaining strong ties to Christian friends of both sexes to support their relationship with Christ.

Item #4: Move through each situation asking kids to give a Christian perspective on each. Expect a variety of answers here. Ask the group which ones Christians might handle differently than non-Christians.

Item #5: Here is your opportunity at taking a shot at answering all the questions that have been piling up during the TalkSheet discussion.

Item #6: The community-building passages focus on our responsibilities toward each other. Read the passages and have the young people share how they relate to a Christian's relationship with the opposite sex.

To Close the Session:

Wrap up the session by talking about ways your kids can have opposite sex friendships without those relationships turning romantic. You may want to take the time to role-play sticky situations like those found in Item #4 to help build the skills and confidence of the kids in your group. Validate as normal the experiences of those kids who are not at all interested in the opposite sex.

Outside Activity:

Ask a panel of people that includes parents, high school and college age students, and some grandparents to attend a session with your group where they answer all the questions the kids ask.

BEGINNING OF THE END?

1 When I think about the second coming of Christ, I feel . . .
(Circle those that apply.)

Excited	**Depressed**	**Sad**
Relieved	**Scared**	**Indifferent**
Cheated	**At peace**	**Worried**
Frustrated	**Happy**	**Motivated**

2 If someone asked me what the Bible says about Christ's coming again, I would tell them _____

_____

_____

_____

3 Circle **OFTEN**, **SOMETIMES,** or **NEVER** for each of the following:

a. I worry about the future.	**OFTEN**	**SOMETIMES**	**NEVER**
b. I wonder when Christ will return.	**OFTEN**	**SOMETIMES**	**NEVER**
c. I would like to learn more about Christ's second coming.	**OFTEN**	**SOMETIMES**	**NEVER**
d. I have a good relationship with the living Christ today.	**OFTEN**	**SOMETIMES**	**NEVER**
e. I am prepared for the return of Jesus Christ.	**OFTEN**	**SOMETIMES**	**NEVER**

4 If you knew for certain Christ would return in a month, how would you live your life differently over the

next 30 days? _____

_____

_____

5 Write down three questions you have about the second coming of Christ.

a. _____

b. _____

c. _____

6 Draw connecting lines between the Scripture verses and the appropriate statements.

1. Matthew 24:42	**a. Call on the name of the Lord.**
2. 2 Peter 3:11	**b. Keep watch.**
3. Joel 2:31, 32	**c. While we wait for the blessed hope.**
4. Revelation 3:11	**d. Live holy and godly lives.**
5. Titus 2:13	**e. I am coming soon.**

BEGINNING OF THE END?
Topic: The Second Coming of Christ

Purpose of this Session:

Junior high/middle schoolers are fascinated with the book of Revelation and the end of the world. They are exposed to astrology and fortune-telling games at school and with their friends. They want to know about the future and what it holds for them. As we approach and enter the new century, interest in the second coming of Christ will intensify. A similar phenomenon occurred in history with the approach of the first millennium after Christ's birth. This TalkSheet provides your group with a format in which to discuss the return of Christ.

To Introduce the Topic:

As the group is getting seated, bang on pots and pans, blow a whistle, and generally make a loud nuisance of yourself. Then yell out, "Jesus Christ has returned!" Now ask the group the following question: "What is the first thing you thought of when you heard that Christ had returned?"

The Discussion:

Item #1: Let the kids share their emotional responses to the thought of the second coming of Christ. Remember—never use the Second Coming or other prophecies as a scare tactic.

Item #2: You will hear the young people's views regarding the return of Christ. Talk about the reality of the doctrine of the Second Advent. Point out that immediately after Christ went into heaven, he promised to return again (Acts 1:11).

Item #3: Focus on your group's preparation for Christ's return. What sort of relationship do the kids have with the Lord and with others?

Item #4: This issue focuses more specifically on the last statement of the previous activity. Ask the group to look at the kind of life that God wants each of us to live in light of his return (Titus 2:11-14).

Item #5: These questions can be answered at this time or saved for a later date so that the proper biblical research and study can be done.

Item #6: Ask the young people to read the passages and match them up correctly. Examine the Scriptures one at a time and ask the kids to try to apply their messages personally.

To Close the Session:

Summarize the different points made during the discussion. Affirm the reality of the return of Christ. Point out that Jesus told us in his own words that no one will know when he will return (Matthew 24:36)—but he will return.

Outside Activity:

Invite the pastor of your church to answer the group's questions regarding Christ's return. Some potential questions to get the discussion going are as follows:

1. Why is the return of Christ so important?

2. What will happen when Christ does return?

3. When do you think Christ will return?

4. Why didn't Jesus tell us when he was coming back?

5. How has the doctrine of the second coming of Christ affected your life?

DO CHEATERS SOMETIMES PROSPER?

 1 How many people at your school cheat?
(✓ Check the one that applies.)

_____ **No one**
_____ **Less than half**
_____ **About half**
_____ **More than half**
_____ **Everyone**

2 What do students at your school cheat on the most? (Circle the top two.)

a. Tests and quizzes
b. Homework
c. Book reports
d. Projects

3 Cheating **does / does not** pay off. (Circle your opinion.)
Why or **why not?** _____

_____

_____

4 Is it cheating? Read each of the following statements and decide.

	SERIOUS CHEATING	BARELY CHEATING	NOT CHEATING
a. Copying off of someone's test paper.	_____	_____	_____
b. Writing answers on your arm for a test.	_____	_____	_____
c. Allowing your parent to do a homework assignment.	_____	_____	_____
d. Asking someone sitting near you for the answer to a test question.	_____	_____	_____
e. Copying someone else's book report from last year.	_____	_____	_____
f. Letting a friend copy answers from your test.	_____	_____	_____
g. Telling a friend an answer to a test question.	_____	_____	_____
h. Letting another student help you on a special project.	_____	_____	_____
i. Letting someone copy an answer from your homework.	_____	_____	_____
j. Copying an answer from someone else's homework.	_____	_____	_____
k. Changing an answer for someone when papers are exchanged for grading purposes.	_____	_____	_____
l. Asking someone to change an answer for you when papers are exchanged for grading purposes.	_____	_____	_____

 5 Choose one of the following Scriptures to rewrite in your own words. Rewrite the passage in such a way that it applies to the problem of cheating.

Leviticus 19:11   Psalm 101:7   Matthew 16:26

_____

_____

_____

DO CHEATERS SOMETIMES PROSPER?
Topic: Cheating

Purpose of this Session:

The cheating question confronts the young adolescent squarely in the face. It is during the junior high/middle school years that peer pressure intensifies. Cheating as a means to get by on a test or other schoolwork becomes more of an option. Many young people lack the experience, skills, and values needed to say no to cheating. Take time to involve your group in a discussion of this critical honesty issue.

To Introduce the Topic:

Make up a short quiz about your church to give to the group. The quiz could ask questions like how many bathrooms are there at the church, what was last week's sermon about, what translation of the Bible does the pastor use, what was the theme of the past summer's camp, what was the name of a missionary supported by the church, and so on. Pass the quiz out to every member of the group. Ask specifically that the kids answer the questions by themselves and no talking. Then leave the room for a minute or two. When you return, have them put down their pencils and talk about the quiz. Announce that you will be talking about cheating. Evaluate what happened when you left the room. Did cheating occur and why? If there was no cheating on the quiz, why?

The Discussion:

Item #1: Talk about the peer pressure to cheat. Tell the group that the pressure to cheat increases in high school, and ask them why this might be true. Often it is true because of the competitive academic pressure with college-bound students. There is also more of an attitude to just get by.

Item #2: Research indicates that as the chance of getting caught cheating goes up, the rate of cheating goes down.

Item #3: Ask the young people what they think of the title of this TalkSheet. Do cheaters prosper? How do they prosper? What will happen to you if you choose not to cheat?

Item #4: Many young people are confused about what is cheating, especially in specific situations. Each of these statements constitutes a cheating situation. Some are active cheating (Items "a," "b," "d," "e," "j," "k," "l") while others are passive cheating (Items "c," "f," "g," "h," "i"). Once you have debated each statement, talk about passive and active cheating and point out that both are examples of cheating.

Item #5: Ask different volunteers to read their paraphrased passages. Then talk about each of these passages as they relate to cheating.

To Close the Session:

Explain to the group that cheating is stealing. When you cheat you take something that is not rightfully yours. Now many students do cheat. They take something they do not deserve and often get away with it. In fact, many students let cheaters get away with it. But does this make it the right way to live? Often cheating is rationalized away as necessary to get by in school.

Not getting caught is the prime directive in giving moral direction to cheaters. This loose standard offers young people little moral direction. This sort of twisted thinking will eventually get its practitioners into deep trouble. When you continue to get away with cheating or anything else for that matter, you will keep doing it. Dishonesty becomes a way of life. But people who live like that become that. And they surround themselves with people like themselves. Ask the group to predict where this kind of lifestyle will lead.

Outside Activity:

Ask the group to compose a position paper that states its official position on cheating ("Whereas . . . therefore be it resolved that we, the youths of First Church. . . ."). Ask all the young people to sign it, embellish it with a large gold seal, and post it in a conspicuous place.

THE DIVORCE DOCTOR

Circle five of the following words that best describe how you think most young people feel after their parents divorce.

Relieved	**Angry**	**Happy**
Responsible	**Sad**	**Depressed**
Shocked	**Rejected**	**Guilty**
Fearful	**Confused**	**Abandoned**
Hopeful	**Accepting**	**Lonely**

2 Decide which of the following parent marriage patterns affects teenagers the most negatively. (Check one.)

___ Continuously married parents

___ Parents divorced during teenage years

___ Parents divorced during childhood years

___ Parents separated but not divorced

3 Check the one marriage statement that comes closest to how you see your marriage future.

___ When I am old enough I plan to marry.

___ I will never, ever get married.

___ I plan on getting married, but I probably will also get divorced.

4 Of the following methods, circle the best way to handle a parental divorce.

a. Avoid dealing with what is happening until you are older.

b. Try to find the positive side of what is happening.

c. Actively try to figure out how to best deal with what is happening.

d. Keep your feelings to yourself.

e. Ask for help from people who care about you.

f. Try to get your parents back together again.

g. Spend time with God to understand how best you could respond to your parents' problems.

Decide how each of the following passages of Scripture could help a teenager whose parents are divorcing or have divorced.

1 Peter 1:3 _____

Romans 15:13 _____

Psalm 68:5 _____

Psalm 27:13, 14 _____

2 Corinthians 4:8-10 _____

THE DIVORCE DOCTOR
Topic: Divorce

Purpose of this Session:

This TalkSheet is not about the rightness or wrongness of divorce. Teens are not responsible for marital failure but, unfortunately, they must live with its consequences. This Talksheet helps validate the feelings of kids who are experiencing or have experienced a divorce, as well as give kids whose parents have not divorced the chance to understand and empathize with their peers who have experienced the tragedy of a marital failure.

To Introduce the Topic:

For this exercise you will need five photocopies of a marriage certificate, one frame, and some tape. Place one of the certificates into the frame, poke one with holes, tear one in several places, tear one into pieces and tape it back together again, and save one to be torn. Hold the certificates up before the group. Explain to them that each of these certificates represents a marriage. The framed certificate is the "picture perfect" marriage. The husband and wife care for each other and work hard at keeping the marriage together. The certificate with holes in it signifies a marriage with some problems. There are a few difficulties eating away at it, but so far it has stayed together. The one torn in several places represents a hurting marriage. Perhaps with help it will survive or it may end in divorce. The certificate torn into pieces but taped together again represents a marriage that has been torn apart but is healing. There are scars, but it can still last. Finally, the last certificate should be held up and torn to pieces. This represents a marriage that has ended in divorce. The certificate of marriage no longer means anything. Pass out the TalkSheets and begin the discussion.

Another interesting way to introduce the topic is to write the word *divorce* in large print on a chalkboard or on newsprint for all to see. Walk around the room flipping a coin. Say nothing for a minute or two other than asking kids to call the coin in the air. If they lose the toss, have them sit away from the group. Some in the group may catch onto what you are trying to simulate. After doing this a number of times, explain that this little activity was like marriage and divorce. In America about half of all marriages end in divorce. (At this writing there has been a small decline in the divorce rate and it can be hoped that this trend will continue.) The people sitting away from the group represent those whose marriages failed. If they marry again, their chance of another divorce is even higher.

The Discussion:

Item #1: All of these are feelings experienced by young people whose parents have divorced. This activity gives kids who never have experienced a divorce the chance to better understand what happens. It also lets kids who have experienced the pain share some of it with the rest of the group. Ask several of the group members whose parents have divorced to share their answers.

Item #2: Do not use this as an exercise to judge divorce but rather for kids to share how they feel about their parents' marriages. Keep the group safe by not allowing put-downs of other family situations. Young people will differ in their opinions but all will have one.

Item #3: Use this chance to affirm the importance of marriage and the choice these young people will have with regard to their potential future marriages.

Item #4: Young people have different ways of handling stress. Normally, more direct methods of dealing with a parental divorce are the healthiest.

Item #5: Move through each passage asking for volunteers to share how each could help a teenager whose parents are divorcing or have divorced.

To Close the Session:

Wrap up the session by summarizing the points made during the discussion. Write these points in the form of prayer needs. Then each member of the group can take one of these and pray about it during a closing circle prayer time.

Outside Activity:

Assemble a group of four to five people for a panel discussion on divorce. Members could include a divorced person, an adult child of divorce, a Christian counselor or pastor, and a married couple. Have your group members write down their questions for the panel in advance if possible.

NOT IN THE COMMON WAY

1 Which age group do you feel has the most difficulty handling a personal disability? (Circle one.)

Babies
Children
Teenagers
Young adults
Adults
Senior adults

2 Underline the five conditions below that you feel you know the most about.

Epilepsy	**Diabetes**	**Amputation**
Deafness	**Obesity**	**Cerebral palsy**
Blindness	**Speech impediment**	**Asthma**
Limp	**Paraplegia**	**Mental retardation**
Learning disability	**Cleft palate/harelip**	**Mental illness**

3 Place an **X** alongside those conditions found in Item #2 that you believe young people at your school would be least accepting of.

4 Suppose you live on a planet where people moved around by flying, but you could not fly. Answer the following questions.

a. How might the people of this planet treat you?

_____

_____

b. How might you feel about yourself because you could not fly?

_____

_____

c. If you were invited to a Christian youth group, how might you be treated?

_____

_____

5 The apostle Paul had a disability. The Bible implies Paul's disability in 2 Corinthians 12:7. In Galatians 6:11 the Bible gives a more specific hint regarding Paul's "thorn in the flesh." Paul probably had some sort of eye disorder or disease that blurred his vision. When he signed his letters written by a secretary, he had to use very large letters in order to read the signature. Paul says he pleaded with the Lord to take away this problem but the Lord had a different plan. Read God's plan for Paul and his disability in 2 Corinthians 12:9.

How is a disability in today's world a chance to experience God's grace and power?

_____

_____

_____

Date Used: _____   Group: _____

NOT IN THE COMMON WAY
Topic: Disabilities

Purpose of this Session:

People with disabilities often scare young adolescents. Because they are coming to grips with bodily changes they themselves do not understand, the sight of anything that does not conform to the norm can confuse and frighten them. Many times they will make fun of people with disabilities as a means of coping with their own fear and confusion. This TalkSheet offers the opportunity to discuss what it means to have a disability as well as a proper Christian response.

To Introduce the Topic:

Write the following words on a chalkboard or on newsprint: *defective*, *crippled*, *handicapped*, *afflicted*, and *deformed*. Have the kids describe the message they get from each of these words. Other words sometimes used unfortunately to describe those with disabilities are *the infirmed*, *shut-in*, and *disabled*. Point out to the group that we need to refer to "people with disabilities" rather than to "the disabled," "the handicapped," or "the crippled."

The Discussion:

Item #1: Ask the group why each age group might have difficulty. Discuss the myth that "disability equals inability," which is simply not true. Another myth that can be discussed here is that people with disabilities are more unhappy than people without disabilities.

Item #2: Many young people are not informed concerning these conditions. Take time to define each of these. Information can go a long way in helping young people become more compassionate and caring.

Item #3: Brainstorm how Christians can influence others to be more accepting of those with disabilities. Ask the group to identify how the attitudes and actions of people without disabilities handicap people with disabilities. Have the group identify the ways people with disabilities are like everyone else.

Item #4: This is a simulation activity that gives your group members a disability and asks them to react to it. Ask the group to answer the questions, then relate the activity to the everyday disabilities with which your group members are familiar.

Item #5: The Lord's response to Paul is contrary to the thinking of our postmodern world. The world could not understand how power comes through weakness, yet that is God's message. We can be thankful for our disabilities because God can work through them to demonstrate his power. Additional Scripture: Isaiah 40:31; 2 Corinthians 1:3, 4; and Ephesians 3:16, 17.

To Close the Session:

The following points can help you in wrapping up the session.

1. People with disabilities are people. They are not patients; they are not sick.
2. People with disabilities need to be treated with dignity and respect. Too often they are treated like objects. We talk for them or at them, not with them. We do not need to do for them what they can do for themselves.
3. All of us have disabilities. We are all limited in one or more ways. Some of us have more severe disabilities than others.
4. Disabilities like mental retardation are not contagious. You do not catch them like the flu.
5. Disability does not equal inability.
6. Christ died for all people.
7. Christ has called all Christians to a higher calling of compassion and redemption.

Outside Activity:

Have a panel of people come to answer questions regarding disabilities. The panel members should include a diverse group—a parent whose child has a disability, a nurse who works with people who have disabilities, a Christian who has lived with a disability, and the like.

FEEL BADS

1 Compared with most people my age . . . (Check one.)

___ **I feel bad more than most people my age.**

___ **I feel bad about the same amount as most people my age.**

___ **I feel bad less often than most people my age.**

2 Complete the following sentence: **When I feel bad, I usually . . .** _____

_____

_____

3 Check the following events that have happened to you in the last six months or so.

___ Argued with a parent about rules.
___ Was bored.
___ Argued with a friend.
___ Moved to a different school.
___ Had a conflict with a teacher.
___ Did not finish homework.
___ Fought with a parent.
___ Felt left out of the youth group.
___ Was grounded or restricted.
___ Was not good enough for a sport.
___ Moved.
___ Arrived late for school or a class.
___ Felt pressured to succeed.
___ Received a bad report card.

___ Felt far away from God.
___ Broke up with a boyfriend/girlfriend.
___ Was bigger or smaller than most people my own age.
___ Missed church or church-related activities.
___ Parents separating or divorcing.
___ Parents fought in front of me.
___ Received a bad grade on a test.
___ Realized that my body is changing.
___ Felt underweight or overweight.
___ Was pressured to do something I knew was wrong.
___ Was not allowed to look or dress the way I wished.
___ Did not have enough time with a parent.
___ Felt rejected by a group of people my age.

4 Underline the events in Item #3 that have happened to you that were negative.

5 Which of the events in Item #3 that have happened to you were positive? Add additional things to the list that were positive life events but that made you feel bad.

_____   _____   _____

_____   _____   _____

_____   _____   _____

6 Choose one of the following Scriptures to rewrite in your own words.

Psalm 42:5, 6   Isaiah 41:10   Matthew 11:28-30   1 Peter 1:3-5

_____

_____

_____

FEEL BADS
Topic: Feeling Bad

Purpose of this Session:

Young teenagers live on the edge of change. Their bodies and minds are growing; their friend and family relationships are shifting. Adolescents experience many events that create change in their lives. These life circumstances can and often do create stress in young people, often making them feel bad. Even positive circumstances can create stress in our lives, leaving bad feelings. Take this opportunity to talk about some of life's events, how they make us feel bad, and what Christians can do about them.

To Introduce the Topic:

For this activity you will need to write the following statements on separate slips of paper. If you have more than ten kids, repeat the statements. Hand out a piece of paper to each group member. Tell them that they need to assume the statements are true in their lives and they are very upset and depressed by what has happened. They are to mingle among the group, look depressed, and talk about why they are feeling bad (what is on their slips of paper). See who can look the most depressed. After a minute or two, stop the mingling. Ask the students how much sympathy they received. Announce you will be discussing life events that make us feel down and out, and hand out the TalkSheets.

1. "Your cat was run over by a skateboard."
2. "You just broke a fingernail."
3. "Your mom threw your baby blanket away."
4. "You just found out there is no tooth fairy."
5. "You found out your best friend is really a werewolf."
6. "Your baby pictures were published in the school newspaper."
7. "You are addicted to baby food."
8. "Your dad won't take the training wheels off your bike."
9. "Your mom got the job as principal of your school."
10. "You can't stop picking your nose no matter how hard you try."

Another simple way to introduce this topic is through poetry. Break into groups of three. Give each group a sheet of paper and a pencil. Instruct the groups to write a poem about feeling bad. Set a time limit and have the groups read their poems to each other.

The Discussion:

Item #1: Most young people will report that they feel bad about as often as or less often than most people their age. Be sensitive to those kids who say they feel bad more than most people their age. You will want to make a mental note of these young people and try to provide assistance to them later.

Item #2: Create a master list of all the things your group members do when they feel bad. Split the list into healthy and unhealthy responses. During your closure time you can go back and add more positive responses to the list.

Item #3: Let kids share the life events that have happened to them over the past six months. Ask the group to make some observations about the sharing, like "the more that has happened to a person, the more likely he or she is to feel bad."

Item #4: Discuss how common "feel bads" are in everyone's life. Ask the group how Christians can respond to the life events that stress and depress all of us.

Item #5: Ask the young people to share their life events. Point out that positive experiences can be "feel bads." Elijah experienced some positive life events that were "feel bads" for him (1 Kings 19).

Item #6: Ask several young people to share their paraphrased Scriptures and try to apply them to today.

To Close the Session:

1. Christians will experience "feel bads" just like everyone else.
2. Christians will feel down because of life's circumstances.
3. Discouragement and depression do not have to overwhelm Christians. Psalm 43 and 55 speak of the hope we have.
4. Christians can fix their hope on the Lord. We may sometimes worry and grow weary over the details of life, but we serve a God who is in control.
5. Be a listener when your friends experience the "feel bads" of life. Both Elijah and Job had friends who supported them when they were down.

Outside Activities:

1. Ask a Christian counselor to attend your group session to talk with the group about life stressors, change, loss, and depression.

2. Ask the group to search the Bible for passages related to hope and comfort.

WHERE DO WE GO FROM HERE?

1 Write a word you think best describes heaven and a word you think best describes hell.

HEAVEN: _____   HELL: _____

2 I think about heaven . . . (Check ✓ one.)

___ Too much
___ Quite often
___ Sometimes
___ Hardly ever

I think about hell . . . (Check ✓ one.)

___ Too much
___ Quite often
___ Sometimes
___ Hardly ever

3 Do you **AGREE** or **DISAGREE** with the following statements?

	AGREE	DISAGREE
a. Science has proven there is no heaven or hell.	_____	_____
b. People who live good lives will go to heaven.	_____	_____
c. Hell will not be as bad a place as preachers make it out to be.	_____	_____
d. It is easier to imagine a hell than a heaven.	_____	_____
e. Talking about hell will scare people into wanting to know more about how to go to heaven.	_____	_____
f. Christians should be more worried about the here and now rather than the afterlife.	_____	_____

4 Try to answer the following question: **What will life be like in heaven?**

_____

_____

_____

5 The Bible does not tell us as much as we want to know about heaven or hell. Yet it does confirm that they both exist and that people will occupy both. "Then they will go away to eternal punishment, but the righteous to eternal life" (Matthew 25:46). The following verses give us a slice of what heaven and hell will be like. After each verse write a word or a phrase that describes either heaven or hell.

HELL

Matthew 8:12 _____

Philippians 3:19 _____

2 Thessalonians 1:8, 9 _____

Revelation 21:8 _____

HEAVEN

Psalm 123:1 _____

John 14:2 _____

Philippians 3:20, 21 _____

Revelation 21:4 _____

WHERE DO WE GO FROM HERE?
Topic: Heaven and Hell

Purpose of this Session:

Talk show interview guests claim to have died and seen the afterlife. Magazines write about people who claim they have lived before and will do so again. Opinion polls report people's views regarding the afterlife. All of this can be confusing to a young person's view of heaven and hell. This TalkSheet encourages a group examination of both heaven and hell.

To Introduce the Topic:

Break into groups of three to four and assign each group the task of creating either a music video about heaven or a music video about hell. Each group must decide what visual images will appear, who will be the stars, and what music will be featured on the heaven or hell music videos.

Another introductory activity would be to take an imaginary skateboard trip through heaven and hell. Begin in hell and then move through heaven. Ask the kids to describe what they might see on their trip.

The Discussion:

Item #1: Allow group members to share their words describing heaven and hell.

Item #2: Young adolescents have reached a stage in their cognitive development where they have the ability for reflective thought. With this ability comes a new perspective to their spiritual beliefs. Thoughts of death and hell often leave them fearful and preoccupied with thinking about the condition of their souls. Take this time to let kids express their joys and fears as well as ask questions about the afterlife. Many of them may have questions about reincarnation and other secular viewpoints that they have heard through friends or the mass media.

Item #3: Take a poll on each of these issues and discuss each one. Ask the students to explain their views and give biblical support for their answers where appropriate.

Item #4: Let kids picture what it will be like to be with God.

Item #5: The Bible does not tell us everything we would like to know about heaven and hell, but it does give us glimpses of both. And it describes both as real places. Ask the group members to share their glimpses of heaven and hell.

To Close the Session:

We cannot talk about heaven without talking about hell and vice versa. The Bible tells us that both are real and both are required. What God has given to us is a choice. When kids ask why would a loving God condemn anyone to hell, they are asking the wrong question. The real question is why would anyone want to reject God's love? God wants everyone to experience eternal life with him (John 5:24; 2 Peter 3:9). Each of us is bound for one or the other (Ecclesiastes 12:13, 14).

Outside Activity:

Ask the students to interview senior adults in your church about their feelings toward heaven and hell. Have them compare their own views with the views expressed by their elders.

R.O.C.K.

1

List your school's favorite rock groups.

a. _____

b. _____

c. _____

2

Where do you stand?

a. I listen to rock music because I like the beat.	THAT'S ME	THAT'S NOT ME
b. Rock music makes me feel good.	THAT'S ME	THAT'S NOT ME
c. I listen to rock music every day.	THAT'S ME	THAT'S NOT ME
d. I read rock music magazines.	THAT'S ME	THAT'S NOT ME
e. I watch rock music videos.	THAT'S ME	THAT'S NOT ME
f. I have attended a secular rock concert.	THAT'S ME	THAT'S NOT ME
g. The lyrics of rock music don't affect me.	THAT'S ME	THAT'S NOT ME

3

Do you **AGREE** or **DISAGREE**?

	AGREE	DISAGREE
a. There is more good than bad in rock music.	_____	_____
b. Parents should have a say in the kinds of rock music listened to by their kids.	_____	_____
c. Rock music is inspired by the Devil.	_____	_____
d. Adults should not protect kids from rock music.	_____	_____
e. Rock music is a good source of information about life.	_____	_____
f. Rock concerts should be rated like movies.	_____	_____

4

a. I can talk with my parents about the rock songs I like. (Circle one.)

Every song   **Some songs**   **No songs**

b. I can talk with my parents about the music videos I like. (Circle one.)

Every video   **Some videos**   **No videos**

5

Read **Galatians 5:19-21** and write down which of the behaviors described also applies to the world of rock music.

_____

_____

_____

R.O.C.K.
Topic: Rock and Roll Music

Purpose of this Session:

Rock and roll is the one phrase that defines youth culture today. It has become an institution separated from all others designed to have an impact on teenagers. Rock music and the world it has created has little or nothing to do with the home, school, or church. And the home, school, and church have little to say or do with rock other than to complain about it or pronounce condemnation upon it. Junior high/middle school young people have already established listening habits. In fact, most of them have already been listening to rock music for several years. This TalkSheet has been designed to create a positive dialogue about rock music among youths and between youths and adult youth workers.

To Introduce the Topic:

Obtain some music from the 1930s and 1940s, taped off the radio or obtained from older members of your church. You could also use classical music. Play the music as the young people arrive for your meeting. Announce that you would like the group to commit to listening to this kind of music for the next month. The group will usually react negatively to your request. Ask several group members why they reacted negatively to changing their musical listening habits. If you have difficulty obtaining any music, simply make the announcement. The effect is the same—although it is more pronounced if you have played oldies or classical music.

The Discussion:

Item #1: The responses to this question will give you an understanding of the diversity of rock bands that are popular with the young people in your area.

Item #2: Responses to the statements in this item will tell you how involved your group members are in the culture of rock music. Usually, the more involved a young person is in the culture of rock, the more negatively she or he has been influenced by rock. Most young people do not believe that their music affects them in negative ways, but they will point out how rock music has affected others adversely. Make a list of all of the positive things about rock music as well as all of its negative effects.

Item #3: Allow time for the group to debate each of these statements. There is no need to spend much time on Item "b" since you can delve more specifically into this issue on Item #4. Focus on Item "e" by listing the kinds of information taught by rock music. The young people can generate the list that will help them see the deceptive values promoted by much of today's rock music.

Item #4: Get a group consensus as to how much the young people are talking with their parents about the rock music they listen to and the music videos they watch. Ask the students how they can involve their parents in helping them make good listening and viewing choices.

Item #5: Many of the desires of the sinful nature described in this passage are true of the world of rock. As the group members share which of the behaviors apply, list them on a chalkboard or on newsprint for everyone to see. Then read Galatians 5:22, 23 and decide how much of the rock world promotes the fruit of the Spirit.

To Close the Session:

There is no quick fix solution that Christian adults can embrace to correct our youths' preoccupation with rock and roll. Slam-dunking kids with Bible verses or bashing rock personalities fails miserably. It is naive to think that rock music is innately evil. There is the good, the bad, and the ugly in rock music. When you offer the group your opinions, talk about these three aspects. Challenge the kids to choose songs that can build up their faith in Jesus Christ.

Challenging questions to ask are, "What happens to you when you listen to hard rock?" "What Christian values does hard rock ridicule?" "When you listen to a hard rock song, are you drawn closer or further away from God?"

Here you have an excellent opportunity to talk with your group about the variety of excellent Christian rock music available to them.

Outside Activity:

A valuable use of your group's time would be to play a variety of different styles of Christian music appropriate for this age group. Many Christian bookstores will loan you demonstration tapes if you tell them what you are doing.

TALK ISN'T THAT CHEAP

1 The term *parent* in the following items refers to all kinds of parents—birth, step, foster, or guardian.

My parents and I talk about the really important things . . .

_____ **too much.**
_____ **about the right amount.**
_____ **not often enough.**

2 How often do you talk about each of the following with one or both of your parents?

	OFTEN	SOMETIMES	RARELY	NEVER
a. School grades	_____	_____	_____	_____
b. Chores	_____	_____	_____	_____
c. Christian beliefs	_____	_____	_____	_____
d. Your friends	_____	_____	_____	_____
e. Family rules	_____	_____	_____	_____
f. Alcohol/drugs	_____	_____	_____	_____
g. Your free time	_____	_____	_____	_____
h. Rock music	_____	_____	_____	_____
i. Church	_____	_____	_____	_____
j. Problems you have	_____	_____	_____	_____
k. How your day went	_____	_____	_____	_____
l. Disobedience	_____	_____	_____	_____
m. Sex	_____	_____	_____	_____

3 When you do have a talk with one or both of your parents, who usually starts the talk?

WITH MY MOTHER	WITH MY FATHER
_____ I usually do.	_____ I usually do.
_____ My mother usually does.	_____ My father usually does.
_____ It is about equal between my mother and me.	_____ It is about equal between my father and me.

4 When you talk about each of the following with your mom or dad, how good are the discussions?

GS = Good, Short Discussion   **L = Lecture**

GL = Good, Long Discussion   **A = Argument**

_____ **a.** School grades
_____ **b.** Chores
_____ **c.** Christian beliefs
_____ **d.** Your friends
_____ **e.** Family rules
_____ **f.** Alcohol/drugs
_____ **g.** Your free time

_____ **h.** Rock music
_____ **i.** Church
_____ **j.** Problems you have
_____ **k.** How your day went
_____ **l.** Disobedience
_____ **m.** Sex

5 Read the following verses and summarize each one of them in five words or less.

Proverbs 15:1 _____

Proverbs 18:13 _____

Proverbs 20:3 _____

Proverbs 21:23 _____

Proverbs 29:20 _____

TALK ISN'T THAT CHEAP
Topic: Parent/Teen Communication

Purpose of this Session:

Talk is something parents and teenagers could do more. Parents fear they cannot talk with their children like they used to. Kids wonder why their folks need to talk so much. Parents feel like they are running out of time to tell their children all they will need to know. Kids think they know it all. Use this TalkSheet time to examine the vital issue of communication and encourage more parent/teen dialogue.

To Introduce the Topic:

For this activity you will need six balloons and six slips of paper. On each of these papers write one of the following statements:

1. Tell the group what you say to your mom or dad to get out of being grounded.
2. Explain what you do when one of your parents wants to talk with you about the birds and the bees.
3. Describe the silliest talk you have ever had with a parent.
4. Assume you could ask your parents any question and they would tell the answer truthfully. Tell the group one question you would ask them.
5. Tell the group how you get big bucks out of your parents when you need it.
6. Suppose for 15 minutes you could talk with your parents about anything and afterward they would forget everything that was said. Tell the group what you would want to discuss with them.

Place one slip of paper in each balloon. Blow the balloons up and tie them. At the start of your meeting, choose six kids to participate in the activity. Tell them to sit on their balloons until they pop. Then each player should read what is on the slip of paper and give his or her response to the group.

The Discussion:

Item #1: Take a group poll of where your kids see their communications on the important issues.

Item #2: On newsprint or on a chalkboard, write down which issues your kids talk with their parents about most often. Do the same for those issues that are rarely or never discussed. Ask the group members to summarize what this says about their overall communications with their parents.

Item #3: Talk about who has the responsibility for communication. Do young people have to wait for their parents? What if their parents do not want to talk or are not very good at communicating?

Item #4: Place the four headings on the chalkboard or on a large piece of paper. Ask the group to share its responses, and then place these under the appropriate headings. Those identified more than once under a given heading can be circled. Stars can be placed beside those that are identified numerous times.

Item #5: List the things taught in the book of Proverbs regarding communication. Ask the students to apply these principles to the way they communicate with their parents.

To Close the Session:

Review what has been said during the discussion. Emphasize what young people can get out of dialogue with their parents (trust, support, and fewer hassles). Close by asking the group members to commit to talk with their parents about one issue found on the TalkSheet. You can have the group members sit in a circle and share their commitments before closing in prayer, or this commitment to communicate can be said in the form of a prayer.

Outside Activity:

Here is an outside activity that will bring together kids and parents in a fun yet meaningful way that will allow the young people a chance to see a parental perspective. Talk shows are a popular form of communication today. The format is simple. You will need four to eight parents as talk show interview guests. Your group members will be the audience. Allow the audience to write down questions in advance to ask the guests. The audience can also ask questions during the program. Choose from your group a talk show host. Allow your group members to come up with a creative name for your show like "Fam Talk" or "The Oprah Donahue Show." Set up your room as a talk show stage with chairs in front of the room for the guests. If you have access to a microphone, provide this for your host. A catchy theme song can be played as the guests enter, indicating the start of the program. Have the host introduce the guests and the topic of the show. Provide the host with two to three sample questions to start off the show. The following questions may be used as sample questions:

1. "What would you like to see teenagers talk with their parents about?"
2. "How often should parents and their kids sit down and talk?"
3. "Why aren't parents more understanding of their kids when they talk with them?"
4. "If you could tell young people only one thing about parents, what would you say?"

HOMOPHOBES

1 Why are some kids called names like *fag* or *queer*?

_____

_____

2 *Homophobia* means fear of homosexuals. Check two reasons why young people at your school might have homophobia.

___ Homosexuals are weird.
___ Homosexuality is contagious.
___ Homosexual behavior is a sin.
___ A person might get a reputation for being a homosexual if he or she was not afraid of homosexuals.
___ Homosexuals have AIDS.
___ Homosexuals hate God.
___ Homosexuals might do something weird to you.

3 **YES, NO,** or **MAYBE SO**. (Write in your answer.)

a. _____ Christians should not talk about homosexuality.
b. _____ Christians should be nicer to homosexuals.
c. _____ Heterosexual sex outside of marriage is just as much a sin as homosexual sex.
d. _____ There is not much that the church can do for homosexuals.
e. _____ Homosexuals need lots of prayer.

4 What would you do if a homosexual sat next to you in church?

_____

_____

5 Complete the paragraph below, using what you learn from reading the Scriptures.

What To Do About the Homosexual

The world says homosexuality is an alternative lifestyle, but the

Bible says homosexuality is _____. God hates what
Leviticus 18:22

homosexuals do, but he _____ for each homosexual.
2 Peter 3:9

Each of us is like the homosexual because _____
Romans 3:22, 23

_____. Christians should treat people who say they

are homosexuals with _____.
1 John 4:15-18

HOMOPHOBES
Topic: Homosexuality

Purpose of this Session:

God has called the church to be a redemptive community. Yet the church is also the defender of moral values. And in a postmodern world with collapsing values, homosexuality presents a thorny dilemma. How can the church be redemptive to the homosexual and still uphold its defense of strong morals? The tendency in most churches is to defend a high moral standard rather than to create a loving redemptive community. So the church becomes the homosexual's judge rather than a helper. Adults in the church for the most part have accepted the church's stand without much debate. But today's young people are growing up in a generation more tolerant of alternative lifestyles. The gay liberation movement began at a homosexual bar in New York in 1969. In 1975, the American Psychiatric Association officially dropped homosexuality as a mental disorder. Today's young people grew up with media exposure about homosexuality like no other generation. Use this TalkSheet to discuss with your young people how Christians and the church can love the individual homosexual and hate the sin of homosexuality.

To Introduce the Topic:

On 3 x 5 cards, print the following labels: "rich," "smart," "good-looking," "a gossip," "handicapped," "athletic," "popular," and "shy." Tape the cards to the backs of the group members. Tell the kids they are not to look at their own labels, but they can look at the labels of others. Ask the group to mingle. As the students walk around, they are to decide with whom they wish to be friends. When they find a label they like, they are to lock arms with that person and continue walking around the room looking for additional friends. The catch is that both people must agree to lock arms in friendship. Once two people have locked arms, they continue the friendship search by reading labels and making friendship decisions. Only the person who is locking arms with you has to agree to the friendship. That person's partner can have a say in the friendship, but the final decision is up to the individual who will lock arms. Again, the agreement must be mutual for the two people locking arms. Let the game progress for a few minutes, then have the kids sit down with their friendship clusters. Ask the group what happened. What did the labels do for your friendship choices? What would have happened if one of the labels had said "homosexual"? Tell the group you will be discussing this issue and pass out the TalkSheets. The first item on the TalkSheet covers labeling homosexuals.

The Discussion:

Item #1: Kids will also name other labels given to homosexuals, such as *gays*, *fairies*, *dykes*, and *butch*. Maintain a level of civility and respectability while doing this activity. Explain to the group that we label what scares us and what we do not understand. Your young people also need to know that some kids may believe the labels.

Item #2: Now that the young people realize that we label people we fear and do not understand, have them discuss their fears. Discuss the definitions of *homophobe* and *homophobia*. What are some everyday effects of these fears?

Item #3: Discuss each of these statements, debating those where disagreement occurs. Focus on the statement "Christians should be nicer to homosexuals." How can we demonstrate God's love to the homosexual? God's grace is the only hope homosexuals or any of us have.

Item #4: Let individuals volunteer their responses. Monitor the sharing to ensure there are no put-downs.

Item #5: Ask different group members to share their paragraphs with the group. Ask the young people how easy or difficult it is to hate the sin of homosexuality but love the sinner.

To Close the Session:

During the teenage years one may have feelings for the same sex even if they are for a fleeting second. This does not indicate the person is a homosexual. There is a mile-wide difference between what we feel and how we act upon those feelings. Some teenagers will experiment with homosexual behaviors. Again, they are not homosexuals. They need God's forgiveness and grace just like teenagers who experiment with heterosexual behavior. When the Bible mentions the sin of homosexuality, it usually includes this sin in with a long list of others. This puts everyone in the same boat, for all of us have sinned. Heterosexual sin is just as much a sin as homosexuality.

Then there are those who persist in their homosexuality. Perhaps it is genetically based or the homosexual grew up in a dysfunctional family. Perhaps he or she was sexualized at a young age. Whatever the cause, homosexuals need to hear that Christ died for them and there is a church available to help them with their sin struggle. Homosexuals do not need our name-calling, our discriminatory actions, or our homophobia. What they need is God's grace. The sin of homosexuality is not the unpardonable sin. The Bible clearly teaches that homosexuality is a sin—a shameful and unnatural act. But the Bible also clearly teaches that Christ came to forgive sin and to love sinners. We can do no less.

Outside Activity:

Ask a group of parents to attend the session and talk about their views on the subject. They can take questions from the group and debate the issue among themselves. Make a list of their areas of agreement and disagreement. The group can then see that this is a tough issue. They can also see that the sin is condemned but not the sinner.

SMUT WORLD

 Society does a good job of protecting young people from pornographic material.

___ **True** ___ **False**

 **AGREE** or **DISAGREE?** Fill in the blank with an **A** if you agree or a **D** if you disagree.

_____ **a.** It is normal for young people to want to look at pornography.

_____ **b.** The more a person is exposed to pornography, the more that person will want to look at pornography.

_____ **c.** Television programming contains visual material that could be considered pornographic.

_____ **d.** The more a person is exposed to sexually explicit material, the less likely that person is to develop a healthy sexual outlook.

 Place a check on the line before the following statement that you agree with the most.

___ **Pornography has a helpful effect on society.**

___ **Pornography has no effect on society.**

___ **Pornography has a harmful effect on society.**

At a friend's house after school, someone calls a "dial-a-porn" phone number and hands you the phone to listen.

What will you do? _____

_____

_____

 I would not rent video movies at a store that also rented pornography.

___ **That's true for me** ___ **It depends** ___ **That's not true for me**

Decide which passage is the most helpful in dealing personally with the issue of pornography. Circle the Scripture you chose.

1 Corinthians 10:11-13   **Galatians 5:22-25**   **Philippians 2:12, 13**

2 Timothy 1:7   **James 1:13-15**

SMUT WORLD
Topic: Pornography

Purpose of this Session:

Pornography is readily available to young teens. Many adults do not define it as pornography, which is one reason why sexually explicit material designed to appeal to one's prurient interest is so accessible to youths. Use this TalkSheet to discuss with your group the issue of pornography.

To Introduce the Topic:

Write the following ways young people are introduced to pornography on a chalkboard or on newsprint:

Computer "porno" graphics	National Geographic	*Playboy* or *Playgirl*
Telephone 900 numbers	Soft-core porn magazines	Pornographic videos
R-rated movies	"X-rated" movies (NC-17)	Hard-core porn magazines
Sports Illustrated swimsuit edition		

Ask the young people to identify the top three ways youths are introduced to pornography. They can add to the list you have created. Tell the group that just as there are gateway drugs (caffeine, nicotine, and alcohol) that introduce young people to mind-altering drugs and the drug world, there is gateway pornography that introduces young people into the world of smut. Tell the group that this TalkSheet focuses upon the issue of pornography. Review the ground rules found in the introduction of this book. Many more young people than we realize have been adversely affected by pornography.

The Discussion:

Item #1: Let the young people share whether or not they need protection and why.

Item #2: Take these statements one at a time and poll the group members as to their opinions. Ask for reasons for each one. Take the time needed to allow for any disagreements. Remember to focus your discussion not on pornographic materials but on the attitudes and behaviors associated with pornography. Your intention is not to sexualize young people but to educate them regarding the dangers of pornography.

Item #3: You can further explore this thought by asking what harm might come to the average teenager who has only casual exposure to pornography.

Item #4: Ask the young people to react to this "tension getter." Brainstorm various creative responses to this situation that help the kids retain their friendship but say no to sin.

Item #5: Most of your kids who rent video movies have watched adults browse the porno sections of movie video rental stores. Ask for their reactions to seeing adults select porno videos for rental. Talk about how the makers of pornography have been able to get mass acceptance of their pornography by calling it "adult entertainment." Ask the kids if this is a good label to give pornography.

Item #6: Have individuals in the group debate which passages were most helpful in dealing personally with the issue of pornography.

To Close the Session:

Ask different young people to summarize what has been covered during the discussion. Emphasize how harmless pornography can appear but how dangerous it can be. Help the young people understand that their initial exposure to pornography may seem innocent, but it can easily grow out of control. Point out that pornography desensitizes its consumers to a healthy view of sex. Pornography distorts the Christian view of love, commitment, and fidelity. It promotes promiscuity and an exploitive view of both men and women. Emphasize the compulsive side of the pornography problem. Involvement begins slowly, but for some people it progresses into an addiction.

Outside Activity:

Ask a Christian counselor familiar with the addiction process and pornography to speak with your group. She or he can answer questions the young people have as well as discuss some case studies. Instruct your speaker that you do not want the case study stories to include graphic examples. Your intention is not to be pornographic in discussing pornography but to talk about the pain and sorrow associated with the victims of pornography.

HARD ROCK CAFETERIA

 Check the following words that best describe hard rock:

__ **Inspiring**	__ **Destructive**	__ **Rebellious**
__ **Emotional**	__ **Loud**	__ **Fun**
__ **Beneficial**	__ **Energetic**	__ **Annoying**
__ **Harmful**	__ **Violent**	__ **Anxious**

 What do you think bothers adults the most about hard rock music?

_____

_____

_____

 Circle the words below that best describe what hard rock songs are about.

Hurting others	**Sex**	**Death**
Evil	**Destruction**	**Satanism**
Killing	**Romance**	**Pain**
Hope	**Suicide**	**Obeying parents**
Family conflict	**Caring**	**Self-control**
Drugs	**Profanity**	**Anger**
Partying	**Loneliness**	

 Circle **YES, NO,** or **DON'T KNOW** in response to each of the following:

a. Hard rock concerts should be off limits to kids younger than 15.   YES   NO   DON'T KNOW

b. Hard rock does not have a harmful effect on kids.   YES   NO   DON'T KNOW

c. Kids under the age of 12 should not be allowed to listen to hard rock.   YES   NO   DON'T KNOW

d. Hard rock songs should be rated like movies.   YES   NO   DON'T KNOW

e. Kids who listen to hard rock are more likely to get into trouble than kids who don't.   YES   NO   DON'T KNOW

f. Teenagers should be allowed to listen to whatever kind of music they choose.   YES   NO   DON'T KNOW

Read **Colossians 2:8**. Then write down one thing about hard rock music that you think could lead a person away from Christ.

One thing about hard rock music that could lead a person away from Christ is _____

_____

_____

HARD ROCK CAFETERIA
Topic: Hard Rock Music

Purpose of this Session:

Young teens are not as familiar with traditional rock and roll music as are older youths and young adults. They have been socialized into a more explicit rock, much of it pushed by harder styles of rock music. This new genre of harder rock has shown little self-restraint as it has departed from more traditional forms of rock music. This TalkSheet offers the opportunity to discuss this newer form of harder rock that is having a profound influence on young people.

To Introduce the Topic:

Arrange to have a hard rock cassette or CD playing as group members arrive. Observe and later point out their reactions. Were they annoyed, excited, or ignoring the music? When the group members are assembled, ask them to name a number of hard rock bands that are popular with kids at their school.

The Discussion:

Item #1: Allow a number of group members to share their words. By doing so, your group is defining hard rock. See if your group can decide what makes hard rock different from other styles of rock music.

Item #2: Give them time to talk but do not allow the sharing to degenerate into a gripe session. At the same time remember young people need to feel heard on this important topic. Quick fix solutions such as condemning the music as satanic are in fact no solution at all; rather they build walls. Kids need to be heard and their opinions affirmed.

Item #3: Take this time as an opportunity to discuss the lyrical content of hard rock. Keep the discussion general to avoid being offensive. Many of the lyrics are quite graphic, violent, and obscene.

Item #4: Take time to explore each of these statements. Item "b" can be explored realistically by asking for examples from the kids. Items "c" and "f" need to be examined by asking at what age should kids be allowed to listen to hard rock and why. Kids usually give their ages as the appropriate age. Item "d" provides another opportunity to talk about the lyrical content of hard rock.

Item #5: Create a list of all the things your group members identified.

To Close the Session:

Young teens usually have well-established rock music listening habits. However, as they grow older they will undoubtedly be exposed to harder and harder rock. They do not have to be passive receptors of any of this music. They do have a choice. Point out to your group members that they do not have to accept the values imposed by hard rock. They can continue to learn more about Christ and his kingdom and use the Bible as a framework for living rather than the values taught by hard rock.

One of the strongest impacts you can have on your group is to simply summarize the points made during the discussion. Hard rock may have had its defenders during the discussion, but if you listened and respected the opinions of all participants, you most likely found most group members openly talking about the negative aspects of hard rock. Reflecting on what has been said by the kids themselves about hard rock music will be much more powerful than anything you could say.

Outside Activity:

Rate a number of hard rock CDs or cassettes like movies are rated (G, PG, PG-13, R, NC-17). Then discuss the reasons why each was given the rating it received.

HOTLINE TO HEAVEN

1 Check (✓) the one prayer pattern from the five listed below that comes closest to describing you.

___ **I hardly ever pray.**

___ **I pray but usually only at church or before meals.**

___ **I pray more than just at church and before meals.**

___ **I pray quite a bit.**

___ **I pray all of the time.**

2 How satisfied are you with your prayer life? (Circle one.)

It's cool   It needs some improvement   It stinks

3 Have you ever . . .

___ **wondered if God was really listening when you prayed?**

___ **felt especially close to God while praying?**

___ **received an answer to a prayer request?**

___ **not wanted to pray, but did so anyway?**

4 People who pray are generally happier than people who do not pray.

___ **True**   ___ **False**

REASON: _____

_____

_____

_____

5 Read **Hebrews 4:14-16** and write down one new thing you learned about prayer.

_____

_____

_____

HOTLINE TO HEAVEN
Topic: Prayer

Purpose of this Session:

Prayer is basic to the Christian life. Young people need to be encouraged to talk and to listen to God. Despite the importance of prayer, many young people spend very little time doing it. Take time to consider this topic critical to Christian growth by having a TalkSheet discussion.

To Introduce the Topic:

For this introductory activity hand out a paper lunch bag and a marker to each member of the group. Have them write one to five-word prayers to God on the bag. Prayers they wish to make public can be written on the outside of the bag; prayers they wish to remain private can be written inside. When the group has finished, ask volunteers to share the outsides of their bags with the group. Make a master list of all the prayers that were shared.

The Discussion:

Item #1: Take a poll of the group to determine a group average. Then use this item to evaluate both the quantity and quality of the average prayer pattern. Give the group average a prayer grade of A, B, C, D, or F.

Item #2: This item can be used to move from a group average to a more personal evaluation. Ask volunteers to provide reasons for their responses.

Item #3: Use this item to share personal feelings regarding prayer. If you share your feelings about each statement first, group members will be more willing and honest in their own sharing.

Item #4: Does prayer have much to do with happiness and the quality of one's life? Many Christians who take prayer seriously say yes! Check out what your kids think.

Item #5: Ask for volunteers to share what they learned about prayer. Have the kids use a Bible concordance to look up additional passages about prayer.

To Close the Session:

Refer to the master list of prayers created during the introduction. Ask different young people to volunteer to take certain prayers. Put the volunteers' initials by the prayers they chose. When all the prayers have initials by them, spend time as a group praying for each one. Then ask for a quiet time of prayer so that the private prayers written on the inside of the bags can be prayed.

Outside Activity:

Your youth group activities calendar can double as a prayer calendar. The next time you create your calendar, print the names of kids and adults involved in your group in each of the daily squares. Somewhere on the calendar provide instructions so that kids understand that on different days they are to pray for the specific person whose name appears. Hand out the calendars and encourage your students throughout the month to keep up their prayer support for members of the youth group.

FIBS, LITTLE WHITE LIES, AND OTHER HALF-TRUTHS

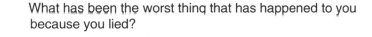

1 What has been the worst thing that has happened to you because you lied?

_____

2 Who do you lie to the most?

___ **Mother**
___ **Father**
___ **Friends**
___ **Teachers**
___ **Brothers/sisters**
___ **Coaches**
___ **Other:** _____

3 **YES** or **NO?** (Circle your answer.)

a. Boys lie more often than girls.	YES	NO
b. It is easier to tell the truth than to lie.	YES	NO
c. You can get more from lying than from telling the truth.	YES	NO
d. Most lies do not hurt anyone.	YES	NO
e. There is a difference between a white lie and a big lie.	YES	NO
f. There are times when a teenager has to lie.	YES	NO

4 Check how **right** or **wrong** each of the following lies are.

	VERY WRONG	WRONG	CONFUSED	RIGHT
a. Lie to your parents about finishing homework to get them off your back.	___	___	___	___
b. Lie to a friend's parent to keep him or her from getting into trouble.	___	___	___	___
c. Lie to a teacher so that you will be given an extra day to finish a book report.	___	___	___	___
d. Lie about where you have been to a parent so you won't get into trouble.	___	___	___	___
e. Lie to a friend to avoid hurting his or her feelings.	___	___	___	___
f. Lie about your age to get into a movie theater.	___	___	___	___
g. Lie to a stranger about where you live.	___	___	___	___

5 Read the five Scriptures below and identify the matching phrases. Cross out the extra phrase.

1. Psalm 5:9, 10	**a.** The Lord hates it when we lie, but he loves honesty.
2. Proverbs 12:22	**b.** God approves of lying when you have to do it.
3. Colossians 3:9	**c.** One of the ten commandments.
4. Proverbs 19:9	**d.** Some people are full of deceit.
5. Exodus 20:16	**e.** Christians are brand new people who do not need to lie.
	f. Bad stuff happens when you lie.

FIBS, LITTLE WHITE LIES, AND OTHER HALF-TRUTHS
Topic: Lying

Purpose of this Session:

Young teenagers lie. And many of them lie often. But this pattern of lying that appears to be a culturally acceptable strategy is contrary to God's plan for living. Use this TalkSheet discussion time to talk about the serious problem of lying.

To Introduce the Topic:

Ask someone in the group to summarize the story of "The Little Boy Who Cried Wolf." Ask the group to tell a modern day version of the story.

Another introductory strategy is to ask the group the following question: "If you were to be hooked up to a lie detector, would you agree to answer any question your parents asked you? How about any question your youth pastor asked you? Your best friend? Your boyfriend/girlfriend?" Then process why they would or would not submit to the lie detector test.

The Discussion:

Item #1: Ask the young people to share the consequences of their lies. Discuss how the negative consequences of lies outweigh any positive benefits.

Item #2: Most kids lie the most to their parents. Talk about why we would lie to the people closest to us.

Item #3: Discuss each statement asking for volunteers to share their answers. Talk about how lying gives one the deceptive feeling of control and power, but this feeling is an illusion.

Item #4: Explore how we rationalize and justify lying. Explain that we often believe our good intentions are reason enough to lie. But God looks at the big picture, which is what we need to do. How do we know our intentions are so good? How can we be sure that our lies will ensure that everything will work out?

Item #5: Ask the young people to read the passages and match them up correctly. Discuss the Scriptures one at a time and ask the kids to try to apply their messages to their own lives.

To Close the Session:

Lying gives us a false sense of control and power. We may feel we have managed a situation successfully but that perception is illusionary. Lying is like microwave popcorn. The little kernels sit peacefully in their package. But when the microwave heats them up, the package grows bigger and bigger. When the heat of daily living is on, we sometimes lie. But like the package of popcorn, the lies grow and grow until finally they become unmanageable.

Outside Activity:

For this activity to be successful, a high level of trust must exist within your group. Remind your kids of the TalkSheet ground rule, "What is said in this room stays in this room." Ask the young people to share lies they wish they could erase and why. The purpose of the activity is to help young people appreciate the benefits of honesty. You can wrap up the activity by talking about those benefits.

HAPPILY EVER AFTER

1 How happy are you today? (Check only one box.)
- ☐ **Very happy**
- ☐ **Happy**
- ☐ **Sort of happy**
- ☐ **Not too happy**
- ☐ **Not happy at all**

2 You have just won $100,000. What could you possibly buy that would make you happy?

_____

_____

_____

3 What brings happiness? (Circle your top three choices.)

A purpose in life	Salvation	Good looks
Helping others	Material things	Good grades
Health	Positive family life	Boyfriend/girlfriend
Popularity	Relationship with Christ	Great friends

4 How do you feel? (Circle your answer.)

a. I would be happier if I were in high school.	YES	MAYBE	NO
b. I would be happier if I looked different.	YES	MAYBE	NO
c. I would be happier if I had different parents.	YES	MAYBE	NO
d. I would be happier if I lived somewhere else.	YES	MAYBE	NO
e. I would be happier if I were smarter.	YES	MAYBE	NO

5 My relationship with Christ is important to my happiness. (✓ Check one.)
- _____ **All of the time**
- _____ **Some of the time**
- _____ **None of the time**

6 Match the Scriptures with the statements on the right.

1. Proverbs 3:13	**a. Christ's joy in you**
2. Proverbs 16:20	**b. Forgiveness of sin**
3. Psalm 1:1	**c. Rejoice in the Lord**
4. Psalm 32:1, 2	**d. Stay away from evil**
5. John 15:11	**e. Trust in the Lord**
6. Philippians 4:4	**f. Wisdom**

Date Used: _____   Group: _____

HAPPILY EVER AFTER
Topic: Happiness

Purpose of this Session:

More than any other age group, young people indicate their desire to be happy. But do young people know what they want? This TalkSheet was designed to discuss this often elusive thing called *happiness*.

To Introduce the Topic:

Give each group member a piece of paper and a pencil. Ask them to draw what they think happiness might look like. When they have completed their drawings, ask several to show theirs to the group.

Another fun lead-in to the discussion is a letter search. On 3 x 5 cards spell out the word *happiness*, one letter per card. Have tape available and designate an appropriate spot to spread out the letters. Hide these cards around your meeting area. Make it a challenge by taping cards beneath chairs, behind doors, under piano benches, and the like. Tell your group that it will be searching for a word that spells out the topic for the session. Explain that when they find a letter they are to bring it to the front of the room and tape it to the designated area. At any given time a group member can choose to rearrange the letters. Once all the letters have been found, ask your group to sit down and pass out copies of the TalkSheet to each member.

The Discussion:

Item #1: Do a group happiness check by polling the young people and computing an average happiness level. Let kids explain their personal ratings. Be sensitive to young people who are hurting.

Item #2: Point out that so often we define happiness by things that can be bought. Many people spend a lifetime trying to buy happiness.

Item #3: Put the list on the chalkboard or on newsprint. Ask the group members to identify the top five or so items that the average young person their age would say bring happiness. Place a square around these. Now ask the group to share those that they circled. Circle the ones reported by two or more young people. Compare the two. Is there a difference between the average kid (more of a secular orientation) and the Christian kid? Why or why not? Which of the things on the list are worth building your life around?

Point out that the things that make life worth living are those things that will bring happiness. There is, however, a paradox here. If one spends his or her life pursuing happiness (which can equal hedonism or pleasure), one will not find it. But if one spends her or his life in service to God and others, happiness will be a by-product. Happiness can never be a goal, only a by-product. Happiness is an interesting concept that people have difficulty defining, but they can tell you when they have experienced it.

Item #4: Often we play the "if only" game thinking that a thing or a circumstance will make us happy. Ask the kids if this has been true in their lives.

Item #5: Explore how a relationship with Christ brings happiness (John 15:9-17).

Item #6: Read the Scriptures and ask the students how each applies to happiness in today's world.

To Close the Session:

Tell the group members that just as they were searching for the letters to spell out the word *happiness*, so, too, many people spend their lives in a futile quest for happiness. Point out that people commonly describe happiness by looking outwardly at things or circumstances. But the Bible says happiness is an attitude. Paul writing to the Philippians said he had learned to be content with plenty or with little. He could do both through the strength given by Christ (Philippians 4:13). Paul had learned to rise above his circumstances because he knew that they could not provide happiness. Research demonstrates that the rich report no more happiness than the common person. Things and circumstances cannot bring happiness. Yet we continue to play the "if only" game believing falsely that changes in our situations will bring the happiness we desire. What Paul had come to realize is something we can learn as well. Happiness is how you view your circumstances, not your circumstances themselves. Paul learned that living under the power of Christ provided him with all he needed to be happy. He quit searching outside himself and turned upward toward God. The Bible calls this joy.

Outside Activity:

Explain to the group that an alien has landed in the parking lot. Okay, so it could never happen. Tell the young people to play along. In the alien's search for happiness, it comes to your meeting and asks the group to explain the earthling version of happiness. Break the group into smaller groups to come up with the best explanation of happiness in terms that this alien can understand.

MOVIE MOVES

1 What types of movies do you most frequently watch (either at the theater or at home with the VCR)? Circle your top three choices below.

Adventure	**Cartoon**
Comedy	**Drama**
Family	**Romance**
Horror	**Musical**
Science fiction	**Sports**
Blood and gore	**Western**

2 Using the rating system found in the box below, rate two movies you recently watched (either at the theater or at home with the VCR).

> **MOVIE RATING GUIDELINES**
>
> | | |
> |---|---|
> | G | General Audience |
> | PG | Parental Guidance Suggested |
> | PG-13 | Parent Caution |
> | R | Restricted |
> | NC-17 | No Children Under 17 |

MOVIE #1: _____

I rate it a(n) _____.

Reason for the rating: _____

MOVIE #2: _____

I rate it a(n) _____.

Reason for the rating: _____

3 How old should a kid be to make his or her own movie viewing decisions? (Circle only one age.)

10	**13**	**16**
11	**14**	**17**
12	**15**	**18**

4 Chris, along with three of his friends, is spending a Friday night at Jason's house. Jason has rented a VCR movie that Chris knows his mom would disapprove of his watching.

What would you do if you were Chris? _____

_____

5 Read **Philippians 4:8, 9** and write what you think it has to say about movies.

_____

_____

_____

MOVIE MOVES
Topic: Movies

Purpose of this Session:

Movie viewing is now a normal part of growing up. The VCR rental movie has made unedited movie viewers of nearly all junior highers. This has taken place in an age where movie rating guidelines mean less and less. What was once rated with an X now qualifies as an R or even a PG movie. This TalkSheet provides you with the opportunity to talk about the kinds of movies your group members are viewing.

To Introduce the Topic:

Hold a movie popularity contest. Create a list with the group's input of the most popular junior high/middle school movies. They do not have to be movies your kids have watched but movies that their peers report to them as most popular. As you read the list, ask the group to vote with its applause. Based upon applause volume, declare a winner and a runner-up.

The Discussion:

Item #1: Ask a number of group members to share the names of several movies from each of their top three choices. This will give you a picture of the kinds of movies your group is viewing. In order to get a parental perspective, ask the group how many of the movies they have watched would win their parents' seal of approval.

Item #2: You may have to explain this activity to some of your group members. The easiest way to do so is through an example from your own movie viewing. The point of this activity is threefold. First, it will help kids become more aware of the reason for a rating system. Ask the group to share some of its ratings. Point out that movies get different ratings because their moral content differs. Second, it will help kids discern good from bad moral content. Ask the group to share the reasons for its ratings. You will get a variety of responses depending upon the types of movies the kids chose to rate. Third, it will help kids create their own Christian rating system. Ask the group to create a list of all the reasons for rating a movie NC-17, R, PG-13, PG, and G. You will get answers like violence, foul language, sex, nudity, and so on. Now challenge the kids to create their own rating system that God would approve of. Apply this new rating system to several of the movies the kids listed in Item #1.

Item #3: Usually kids choose their own age as an appropriate age for a kid to make his or her own movie viewing decisions. Since many of the kids will say they believe they are ready to make their own decisions, ask them if they are making good or bad decisions and why.

Item #4: A common problem faced by parents today is the VCR that belongs to their kid's friend. Many families have adopted much more liberal movie viewing rules than Christian parents. The dilemma that kids face is how to keep their friends while maintaining their Christian stand and abiding by their parents' expectations. Use this "tension getter" to discuss this pressure point faced by today's kids. See if the group can come up with several solutions to the dilemma.

Item #5: Let several of the group members share what they believe this passage says about movies. Compare this verse with the rating system the group created for Item #2.

To Close the Session:

Let the kids know that they do have decisions to make when it comes to going to the theater or renting a video movie. Just because a movie was made does not mean that movie must be seen. Challenge your students to talk with their parents and church leaders about movies before they decide whether or not to watch them. They can also read critical movie reviews as well as apply the Christian rating system created in Item #2. If a movie is bad, they can leave the theater or turn off the VCR.

Outside Activity:

Photocopy and pass out a critical movie review of a popular movie from your local newspaper or a national magazine. Ask the group to read it and decide if the movie is one that is appropriate for a Christian to view.

AIDS ALERT

1 AIDS education at school is . . . (Circle one.)

    a. helpful.

    b. confusing.

    c. boring.

    d. a waste of time.

2 AIDS makes sex scary. (Check one.)

    _____ **I agree.**

    _____ **I'm not sure.**

    _____ **I disagree.**

3 When young people hear about AIDS what do they think? (If you agree, write **Yes**; if you disagree, write **No**.)

    _____ **a.** They shouldn't touch anyone with AIDS.

    _____ **b.** They are afraid to get AIDS.

    _____ **c.** They should make fun of those with AIDS.

    _____ **d.** They want to help someone with AIDS.

    _____ **e.** They feel sorry for a person with AIDS.

    _____ **f.** They are afraid of homosexuals.

    _____ **g.** They want to know more about AIDS.

4 Bill was recently diagnosed as having AIDS. The doctor said Bill was healthy enough to attend school and church. (Circle your answer.)

a. Would you want Bill to attend your school?	**SURE**	**NO WAY**
b. Would you want Bill to attend your church?	**SURE**	**NO WAY**
c. Would you want to be roommates with Bill at summer camp?	**SURE**	**NO WAY**
d. Would you want to be close friends with Bill?	**SURE**	**NO WAY**

5 Decide how each of the following passages can be applied to the issue of AIDS.

Mark 1:40, 41	**Romans 8:35-39**	**Romans 12:2**
2 Corinthians 1:3-10	**Revelation 21:4**	

AIDS ALERT
Topic: AIDS

Purpose of this Session:

Lead your group in a TalkSheet discussion about this topic that is often neglected by Christians.

To Introduce the Topic:

Place the following terms on a chalkboard or on newsprint: *abstinence, hemophilia, heterosexual, HIV, homosexual, intravenous drug user, Kaposi's sarcoma, immune system, monogamous,* and *STD.* Ask the kids to guess what the discussion topic is by looking at the list of words. If no one is able to identify the topic, tell them you will be talking about AIDS or Acquired Immuno-deficiency Syndrome, a disease that attacks the immune system of the body. Then define the terms. You may also want to wait and define the terms as you move through the TalkSheet discussion.

Abstinence—To say no to something. When referring to the AIDS virus, the safest way to avoid the disease is to say no to pre-marital sex and drug use.

Hemophilia—A disease of the blood that requires people to get blood transfusions and blood clotting products. Since AIDS can be transmitted through the blood, some hemophiliacs have contracted the disease.

Heterosexual—A person who is sexually attracted to members of the opposite sex. Heterosexuals can get AIDS just as homo-sexuals can.

HIV—Human Immunodeficiency Virus that is the germ or virus scientists think causes AIDS.

Homosexual—A person who is sexually attracted to members of the same sex. Homosexuals have been at high risk for getting AIDS. The risky sexual behaviors of some homosexuals make it easier for them to get AIDS. But AIDS is not a homosexual dis-ease.

Immune system—That part of the body that protects us from disease. AIDS attacks this part of the body so that it cannot fight off other diseases.

Intravenous drug user—A person who takes drugs with a needle. IV drug users often share needles, which spreads the AIDS virus.

Kaposi's sarcoma—A rare type of cancer that people with AIDS frequently get.

Monogamous—A faithful sexual relationship with only one other person.

STD—A sexually transmitted disease that can be given to someone through sexual contact. AIDS is one of many STDs.

The Discussion:

Item #1: Explore with the students what they have learned and already know about AIDS.

Item #2: Ask the group to explain its answers. Some young people have a distorted view of sex because they have grown up hearing about sexual molestation, "stranger danger," and AIDS. Others believe their youth protects them from the disease.

Item #3: Discuss the group's answers, then talk about a Christian response to those with AIDS. Point out how Christ had compassion for those with leprosy.

Item #4: Talk about some of the myths associated with AIDS. The following are facts that kids need to know.
1. You cannot get AIDS from casual contact like shaking hands.
2. Safe sex is a myth. The best way to avoid contracting the disease is to abstain from premarital sex.
3. You cannot recognize someone who has AIDS simply by looking at them.
4. AIDS is not a punishment from God. If God wanted to immediately punish sin, we would all have been given AIDS.

Item #5: Ask several volunteers to share their opinions. These passages speak about several issues including Christ healing the man with leprosy, a deadly disease during biblical times.

To Close the Session:

Review the points made during the discussion. Point out that AIDS cannot be contracted from casual contact. Focus on God's love for all people including those with AIDS. Everyone needs the Gospel. God wants everyone to accept his free gift of salva-tion (2 Peter 3:9). As Christians we need to take God's love to people who have the disease of AIDS or any other disease. The prejudice shown by many toward those with AIDS is homophobic (born of a fear of homosexuals) and sinful. If God were pun-ishing those with AIDS, then he has made a grave mistake because
babies are getting the disease. All of us deserve death because of our sins, not just homosexuals (Romans 6:23).
   Reemphasize that the best protection against the AIDS virus is not safe sex but abstinence from premarital sex.

Outside Activity:

You may obtain helpful information from your local Red Cross or public health department that can be used to help answer your kids' questions regarding AIDS.